HÄGAR: ROMAN HOLIDAY

There may be some argument about which European first discovered America—an Italian or a Viking. But now the whole world has discovered that jolly Viking, Hägar the Horrible.

Hägar is back with his entire Viking crew plus Helga, Honi, Hamlet, Snert, Kvack and, of course, Lucky Eddie, Hägar's sidekick.

Here's your chance to join the more than 100 million people who "discover" and enjoy Hägar every day, in over 1600 newspapers around the world.

Hägar's creator is Dik Browne, twice winner of the Ruben Award, the National Cartoonist Society's highest honor.

Hägar the Horrible Books

HÄGAR THE HORRIBLE
HÄGAR THE HORRIBLE: ANIMAL HAUS
HÄGAR THE HORRIBLE: BORN LEADER
HÄGAR THE HORRIBLE: BRING 'EM BACK ALIVE
HÄGAR THE HORRIBLE: THE BRUTISH ARE COMING
HÄGAR THE HORRIBLE: EXCUSE ME
HÄGAR THE HORRIBLE: HAVE YOU BEEN UPTIGHT LATELY?
HÄGAR THE HORRIBLE: HÄGAR HITS THE MARK
HÄGAR THE HORRIBLE: HÄGAR'S KNIGHT OUT
HÄGAR THE HORRIBLE: HAPPY HOUR
HÄGAR THE HORRIBLE: HELGA'S REVENGE
HÄGAR THE HORRIBLE: HORNS OF PLENTY
HÄGAR THE HORRIBLE: MIDNIGHT MUNCHIES
HÄGAR THE HORRIBLE: MY FEET ARE DRUNK
HÄGAR THE HORRIBLE: NORSE CODE
HÄGAR THE HORRIBLE: ON THE LOOSE
HÄGAR THE HORRIBLE: ON THE RACK
HÄGAR THE HORRIBLE: ROMAN HOLIDAY
HÄGAR THE HORRIBLE: SACK TIME
HÄGAR THE HORRIBLE: THE SIMPLE LIFE

HÄGAR®

The Horrible

ROMAN HOLIDAY

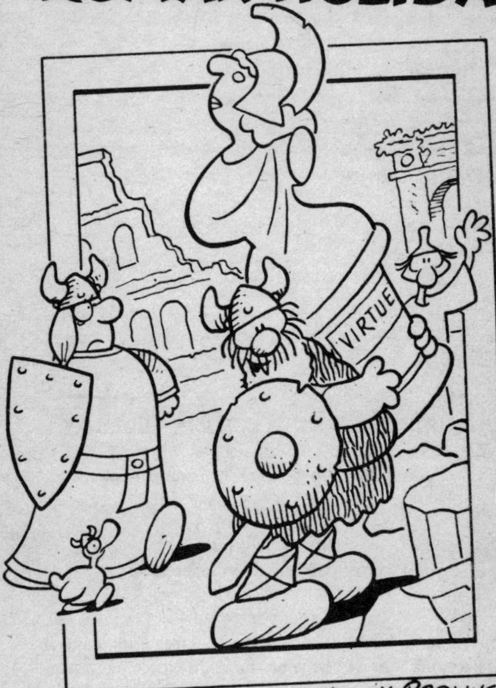
VIRTUE

by DIK BROWNE

CHARTER BOOKS, NEW YORK

HÄGAR THE HORRIBLE: ROMAN HOLIDAY

A Charter Book / published by arrangement with
King Features Syndicate, Inc.

PRINTING HISTORY
Charter edition / November 1986

All rights reserved.
Copyright © 1985, 1986 by King Features Syndicate, Inc.
This book may not be reproduced in whole or in part,
by mimeograph or any other means, without permission.
For information address: The Berkley Publishing Group,
200 Madison Avenue, New York, New York 10016.

ISBN: 0-441-31472-4

Charter Books are published by The Berkley Publishing Group,
200 Madison Avenue, New York, New York 10016.
PRINTED IN THE UNITED STATES OF AMERICA

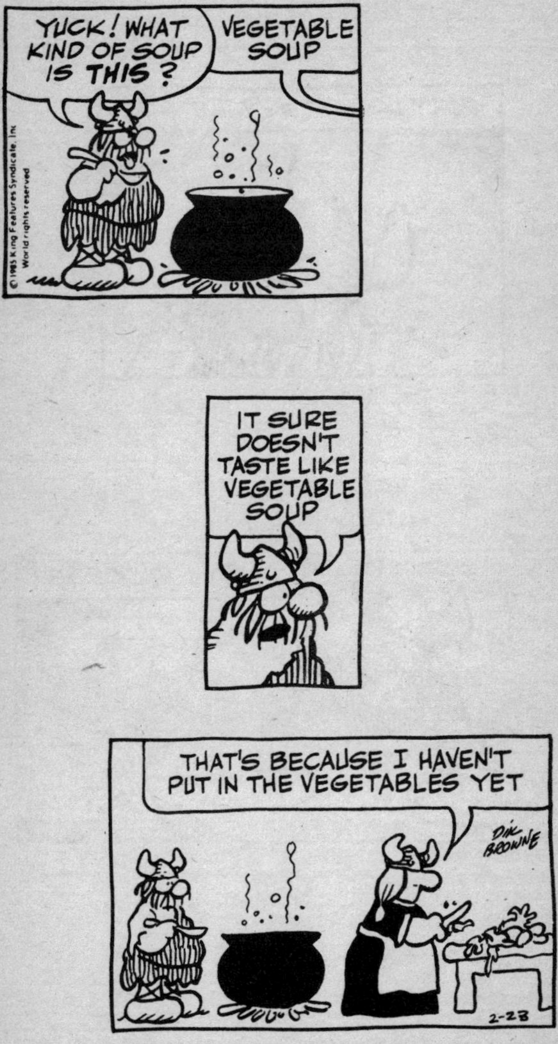
YUCK! WHAT KIND OF SOUP IS THIS?
VEGETABLE SOUP
© 1985 King Features Syndicate, Inc. World rights reserved
IT SURE DOESN'T TASTE LIKE VEGETABLE SOUP
THAT'S BECAUSE I HAVEN'T PUT IN THE VEGETABLES YET
DIK BROWNE
2-23

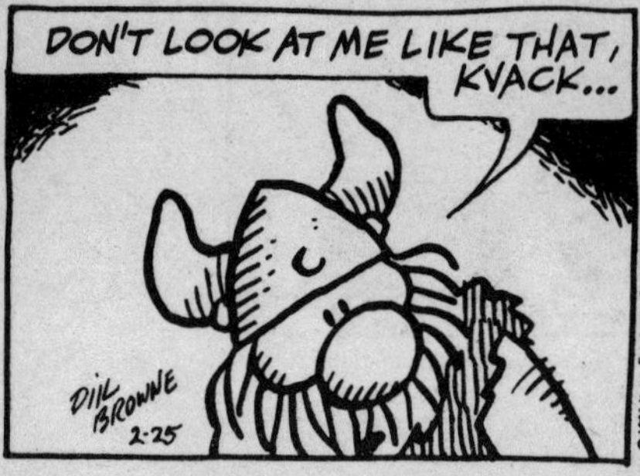
DON'T LOOK AT ME LIKE THAT, KVACK...

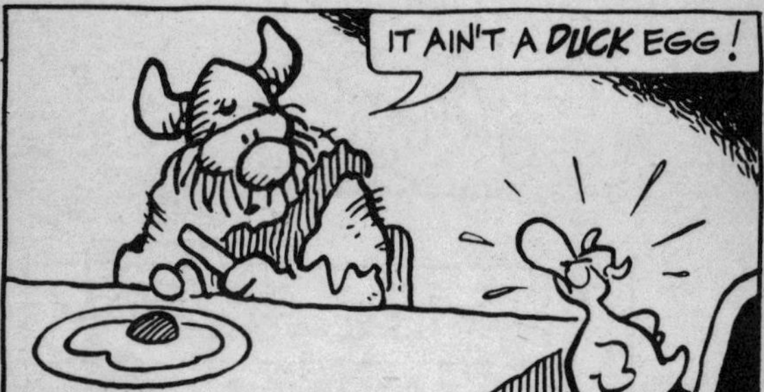
IT AIN'T A DUCK EGG!

GIMME A SHAKE
RATTLE
RATTLE
DO YOURSELF A FAVOR, DON'T ASK FOR A RUMP ROAST
DIK BROWNE
2-26

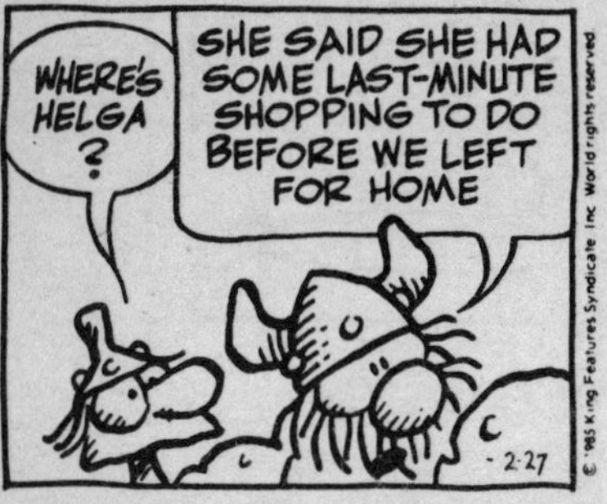
WHERE'S HELGA ?
SHE SAID SHE HAD SOME LAST-MINUTE SHOPPING TO DO BEFORE WE LEFT FOR HOME
2-27
© 1985 King Features Syndicate Inc World rights reserved

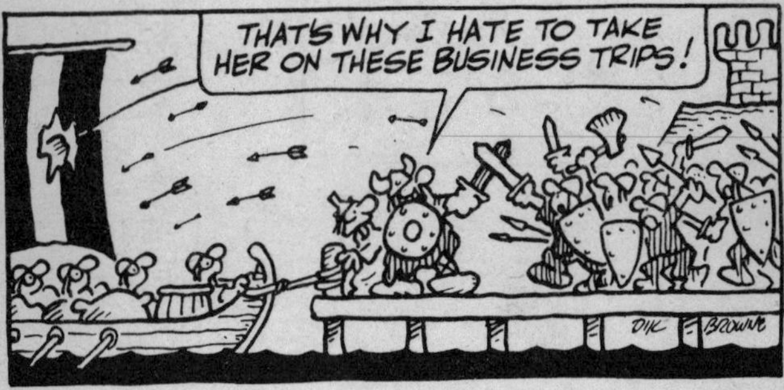
THAT'S WHY I HATE TO TAKE HER ON THESE BUSINESS TRIPS!
DIK BROWNE

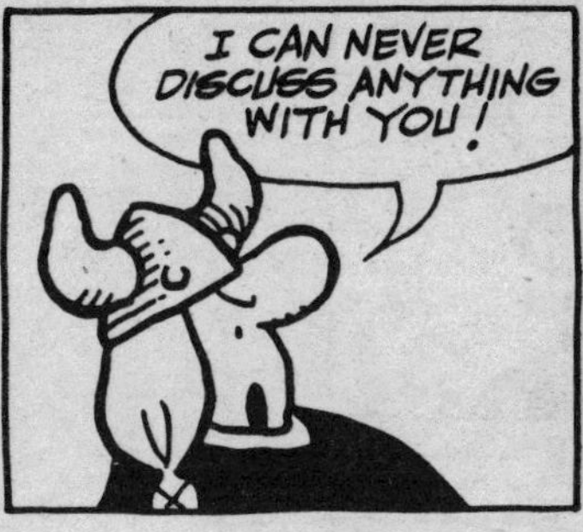
I CAN NEVER DISCUSS ANYTHING WITH YOU!

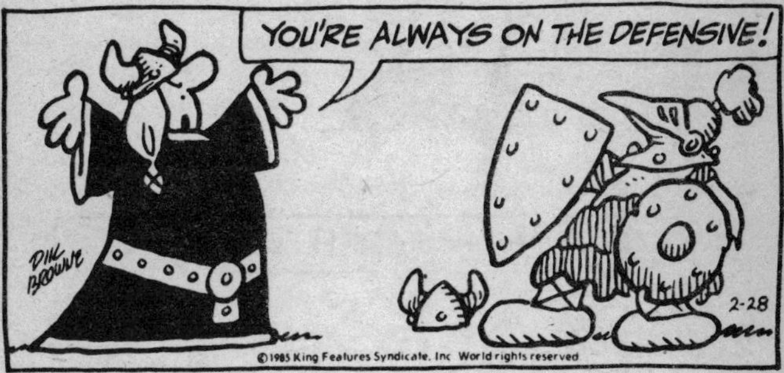
YOU'RE ALWAYS ON THE DEFENSIVE!
DIK BROWNE
2-28
© 1985 King Features Syndicate, Inc. World rights reserved

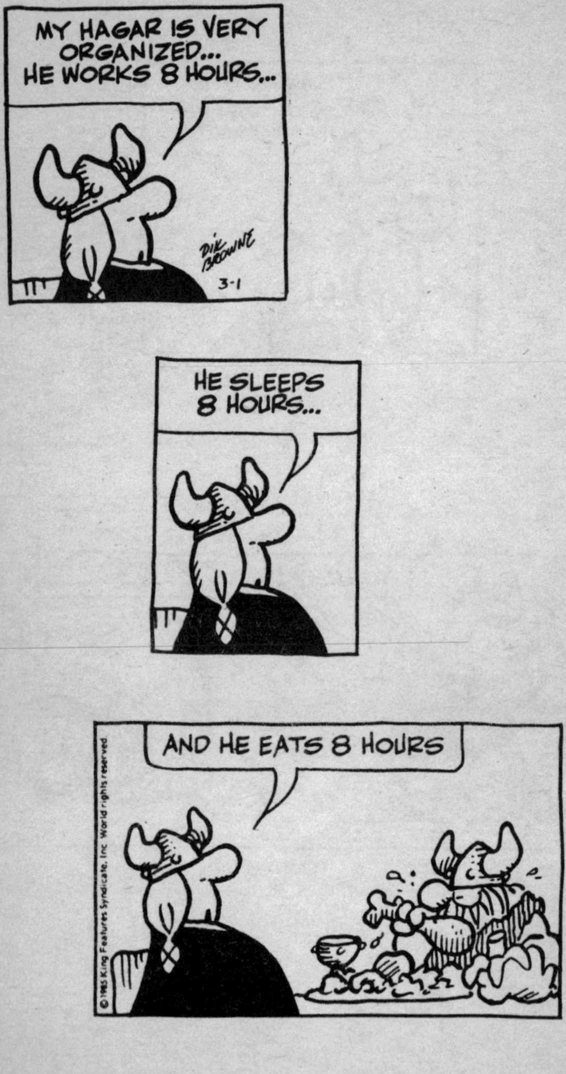
MY HAGAR IS VERY ORGANIZED... HE WORKS 8 HOURS...
DIK BROWNE
3-1
HE SLEEPS 8 HOURS...
AND HE EATS 8 HOURS

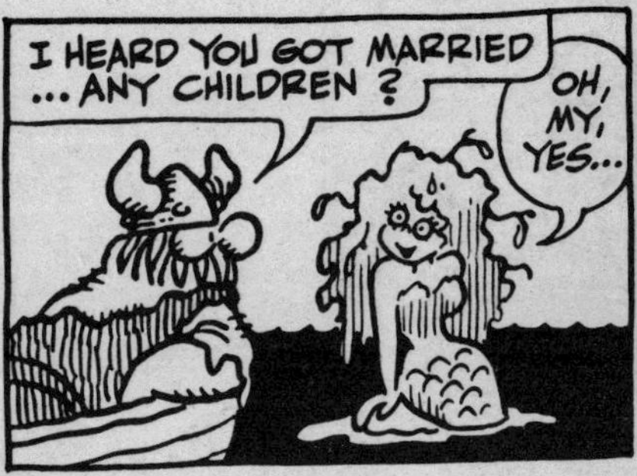
I HEARD YOU GOT MARRIED ... ANY CHILDREN ?
OH, MY, YES...

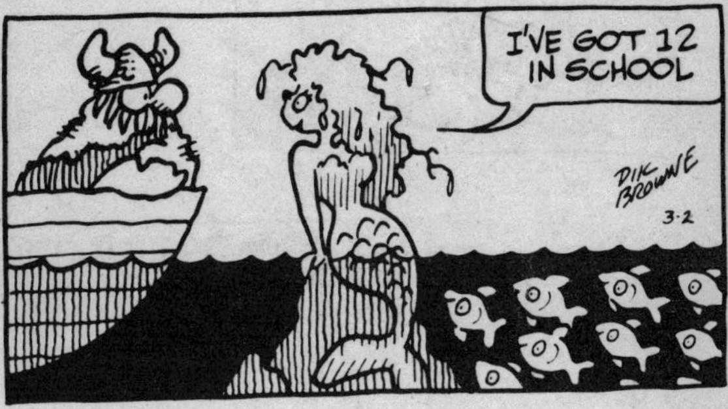
I'VE GOT 12 IN SCHOOL
DIK BROWNE
3-2

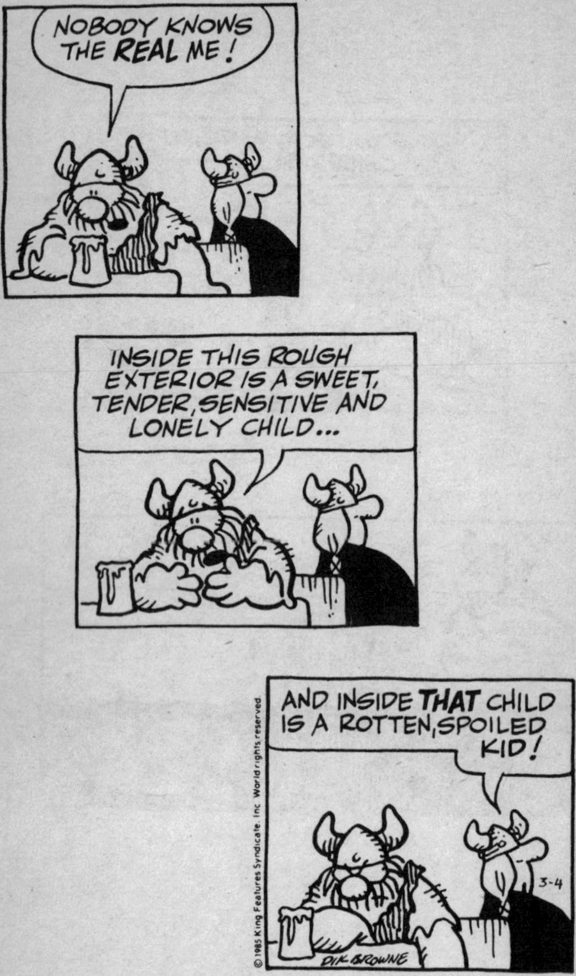
NOBODY KNOWS THE REAL ME!
INSIDE THIS ROUGH EXTERIOR IS A SWEET, TENDER, SENSITIVE AND LONELY CHILD...
AND INSIDE THAT CHILD IS A ROTTEN, SPOILED KID!
3-4
DIK BROWNE

HOW CAN YOU TELL HELGA'S PET DUCK FROM ALL THOSE OTHER DUCKS ?
EASY...
SHE'S THE BAD-TEMPERED ONE WITH THE LITTLE BEADY EYES
3-5
DIK BROWNE
KVACK!
@!!#
KVACK
SAME TO YOU!

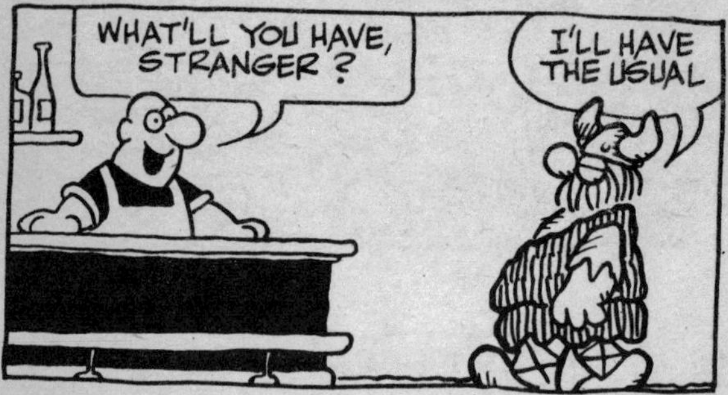
WHAT'LL YOU HAVE, STRANGER?
I'LL HAVE THE USUAL

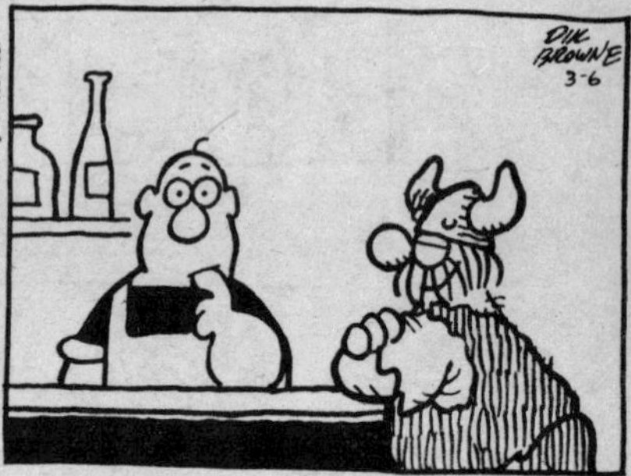
DIK BROWNE
3-6

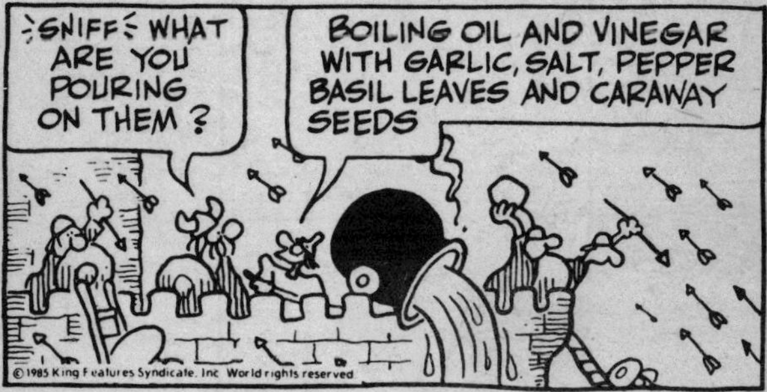

SNIFF WHAT ARE YOU POURING ON THEM ?
BOILING OIL AND VINEGAR WITH GARLIC, SALT, PEPPER BASIL LEAVES AND CARAWAY SEEDS

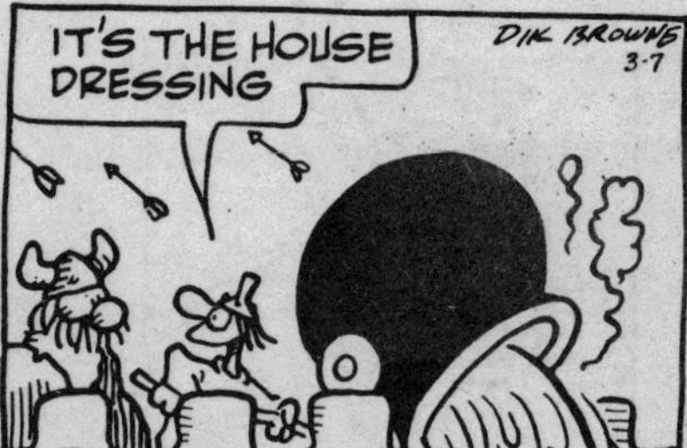

IT'S THE HOUSE DRESSING
DIK BROWNE
3-7

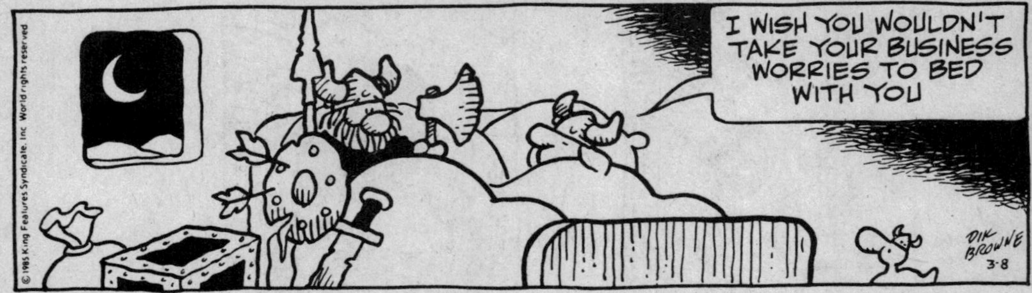
I WISH YOU WOULDN'T TAKE YOUR BUSINESS WORRIES TO BED WITH YOU
DIK BROWNE 3-8
© 1985 King Features Syndicate, Inc. World rights reserved

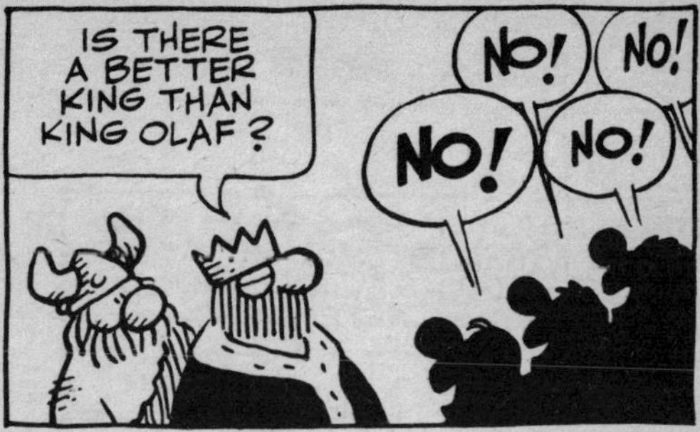
IS THERE A BETTER KING THAN KING OLAF?
NO!
NO!
NO!
NO!

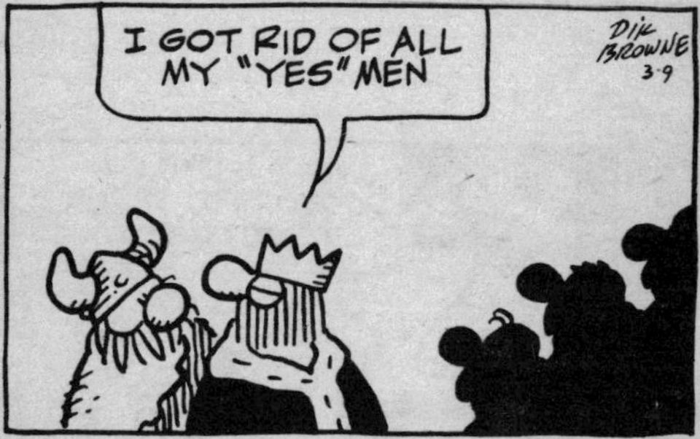
I GOT RID OF ALL MY "YES" MEN
DIK BROWNE 3-9

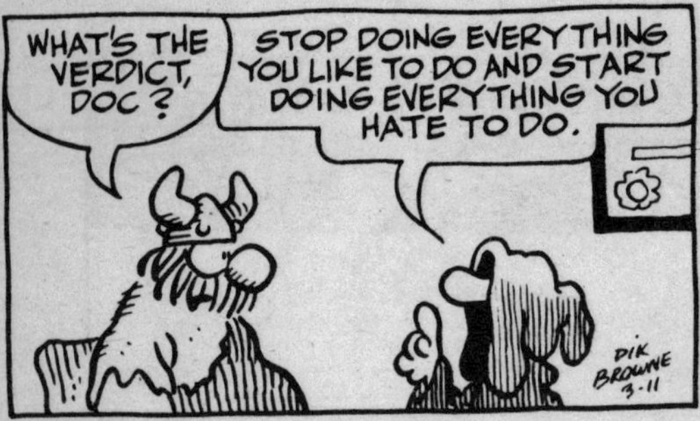
WHAT'S THE VERDICT, DOC?
STOP DOING EVERYTHING YOU LIKE TO DO AND START DOING EVERYTHING YOU HATE TO DO.
DIK BROWNE 3-11

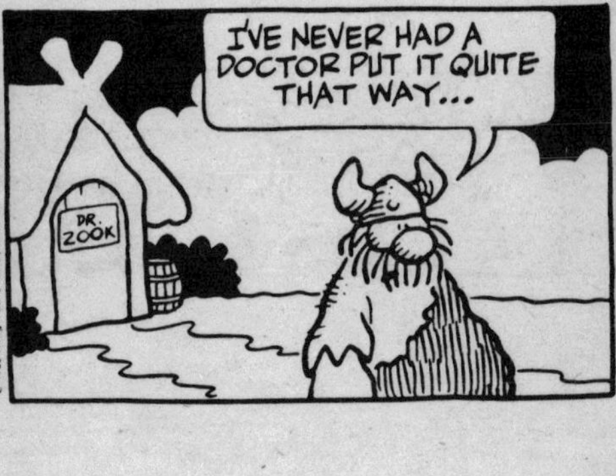
DR. ZOOK
I'VE NEVER HAD A DOCTOR PUT IT QUITE THAT WAY...

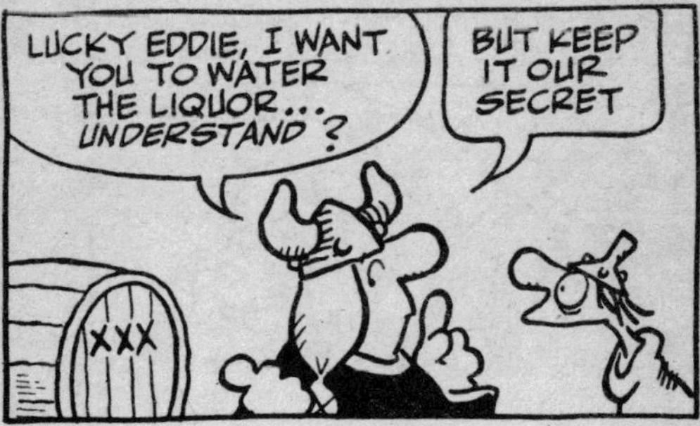
LUCKY EDDIE, I WANT YOU TO WATER THE LIQUOR... UNDERSTAND ?
BUT KEEP IT OUR SECRET
XXX

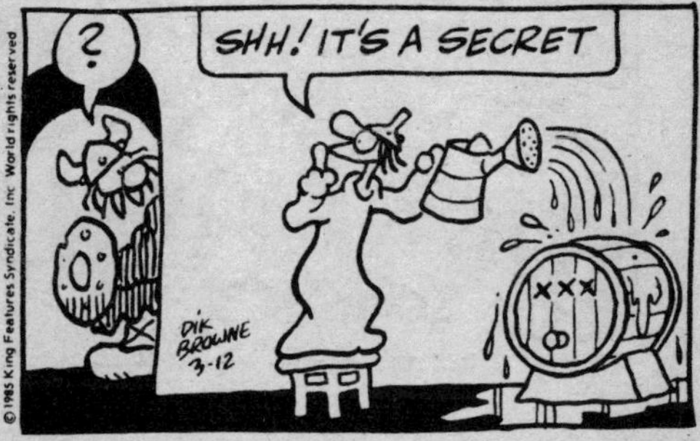
?
SHH! IT'S A SECRET
XXX
DIK BROWNE 3-12
© 1985 King Features Syndicate, Inc. World rights reserved

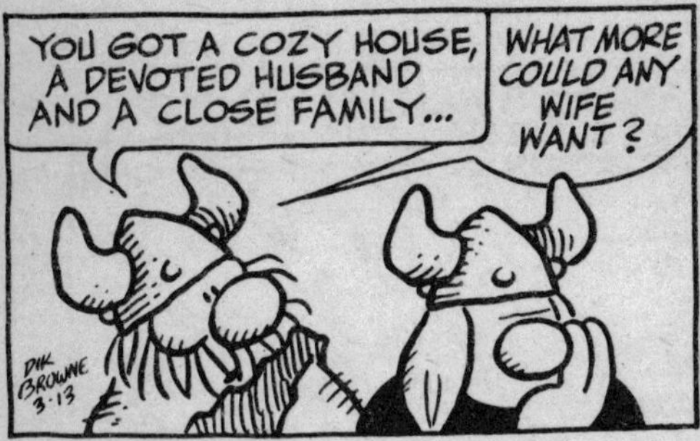
YOU GOT A COZY HOUSE, A DEVOTED HUSBAND AND A CLOSE FAMILY...
WHAT MORE COULD ANY WIFE WANT?
DIK BROWNE 3·13

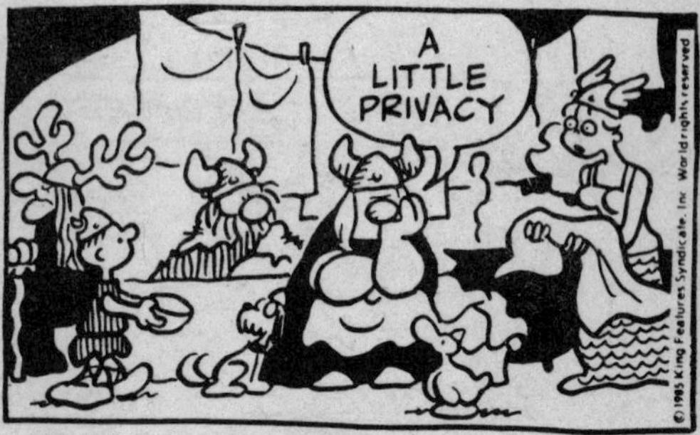
A LITTLE PRIVACY
© 1985 King Features Syndicate, Inc. World rights reserved

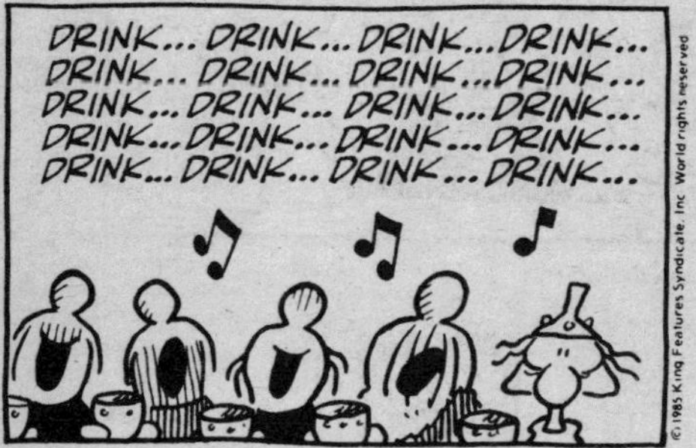
DRINK... DRINK... DRINK... DRINK...
DRINK... DRINK... DRINK... DRINK...
DRINK... DRINK... DRINK... DRINK...
DRINK... DRINK... DRINK... DRINK...
DRINK... DRINK... DRINK... DRINK...
© 1985 King Features Syndicate, Inc. World rights reserved

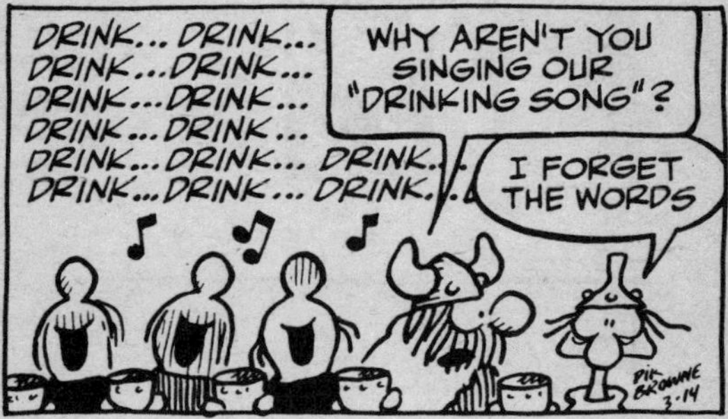
DRINK... DRINK...
DRINK... DRINK...
DRINK... DRINK...
DRINK... DRINK...
DRINK... DRINK... DRINK...
DRINK... DRINK... DRINK...
WHY AREN'T YOU SINGING OUR "DRINKING SONG"?
I FORGET THE WORDS
DIK BROWNE
3-14

MY HAGAR HAS NEVER EVEN LOOKED AT ANOTHER WOMAN
POP!
POP!
DIK BROWNE 3-15
© 1985 King Features Syndicate Inc. World rights reserved

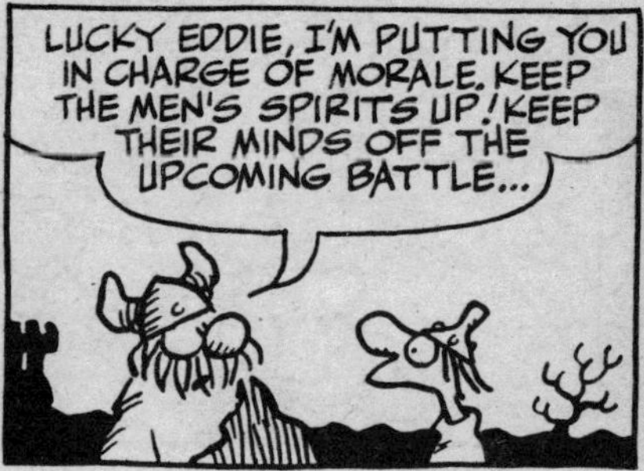
LUCKY EDDIE, I'M PUTTING YOU IN CHARGE OF MORALE. KEEP THE MEN'S SPIRITS UP! KEEP THEIR MINDS OFF THE UPCOMING BATTLE...

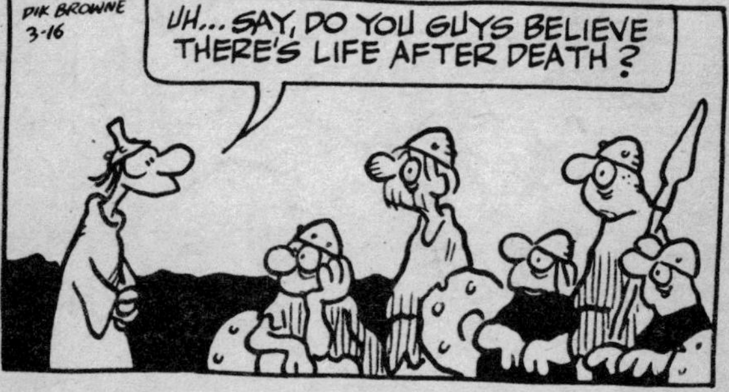
DIK BROWNE
3-16
UH... SAY, DO YOU GUYS BELIEVE THERE'S LIFE AFTER DEATH?

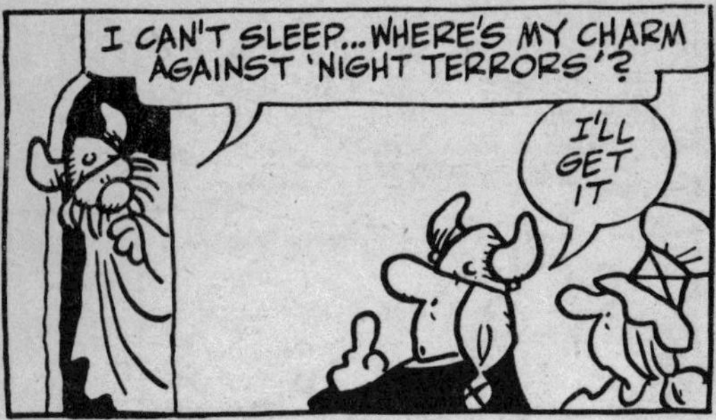
I CAN'T SLEEP... WHERE'S MY CHARM AGAINST 'NIGHT TERRORS'?
I'LL GET IT

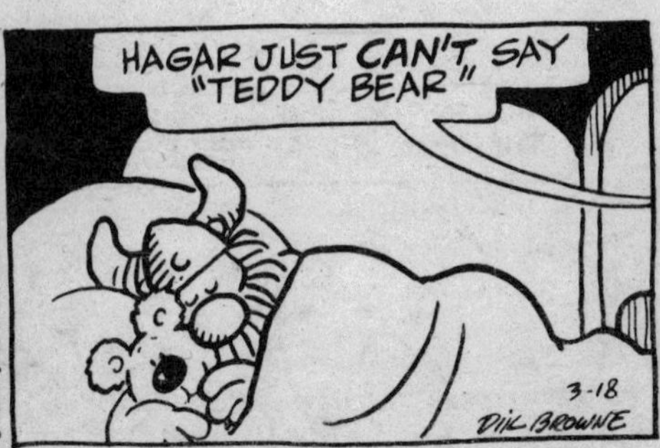
HAGAR JUST CAN'T SAY "TEDDY BEAR"
3-18
DIK BROWNE

I THINK I'LL HAVE A MARTINI!
THIS IS A TOUGH PLACE! DON'T ORDER IT ON THE ROCKS!
WHY NOT?
THEY SERVE IT ON REAL ROCKS!
DIK BROWNE 3-19
© 1985 King Features Syndicate, Inc. World rights reserved.

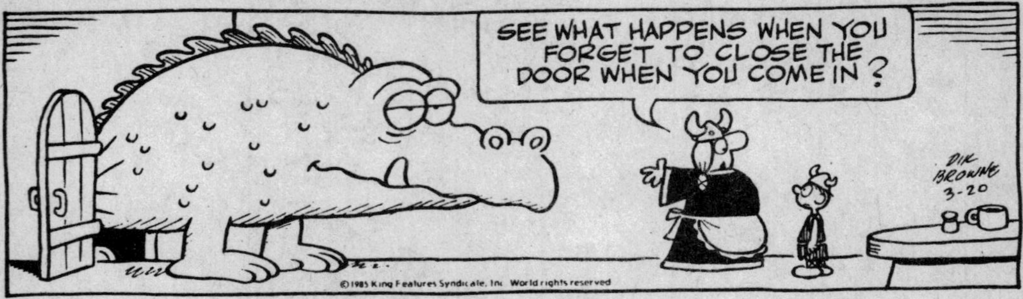
SEE WHAT HAPPENS WHEN YOU FORGET TO CLOSE THE DOOR WHEN YOU COME IN?
DIK BROWNE 3-20
©1985 King Features Syndicate, Inc. World rights reserved

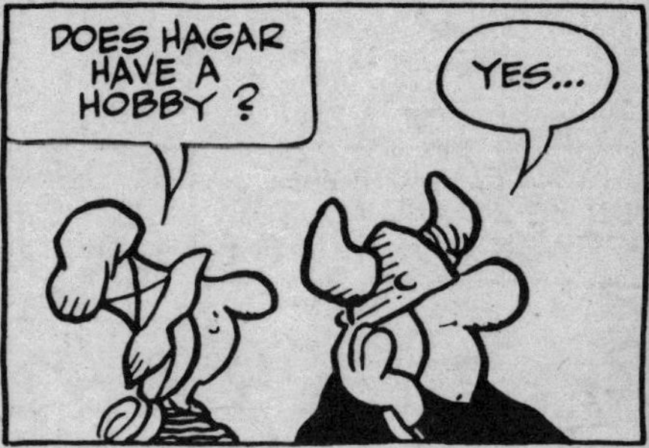
DOES HAGAR HAVE A HOBBY ?
YES...

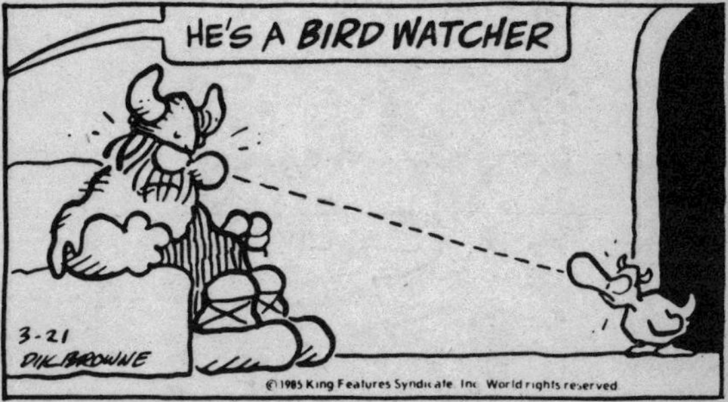
HE'S A BIRD WATCHER
3-21
DIK BROWNE
© 1985 King Features Syndicate, Inc. World rights reserved.

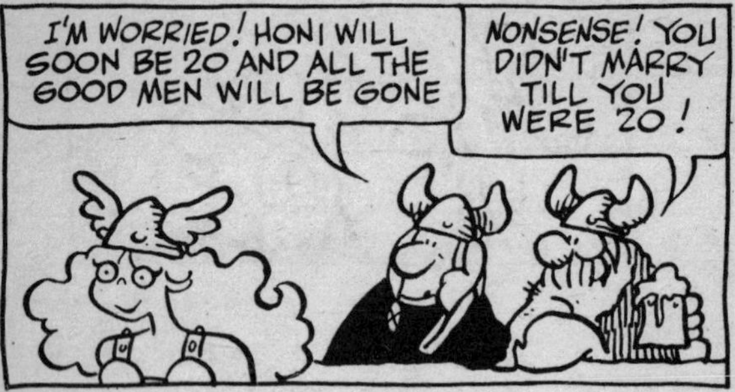
I'M WORRIED! HONI WILL SOON BE 20 AND ALL THE GOOD MEN WILL BE GONE
NONSENSE! YOU DIDN'T MARRY TILL YOU WERE 20!

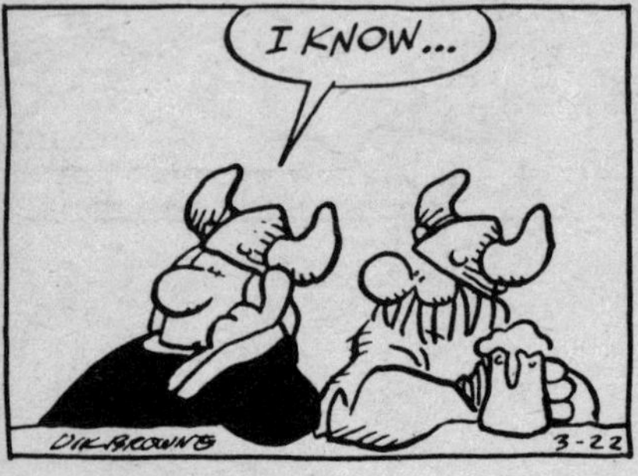
I KNOW...
DIK BROWNE
3-22

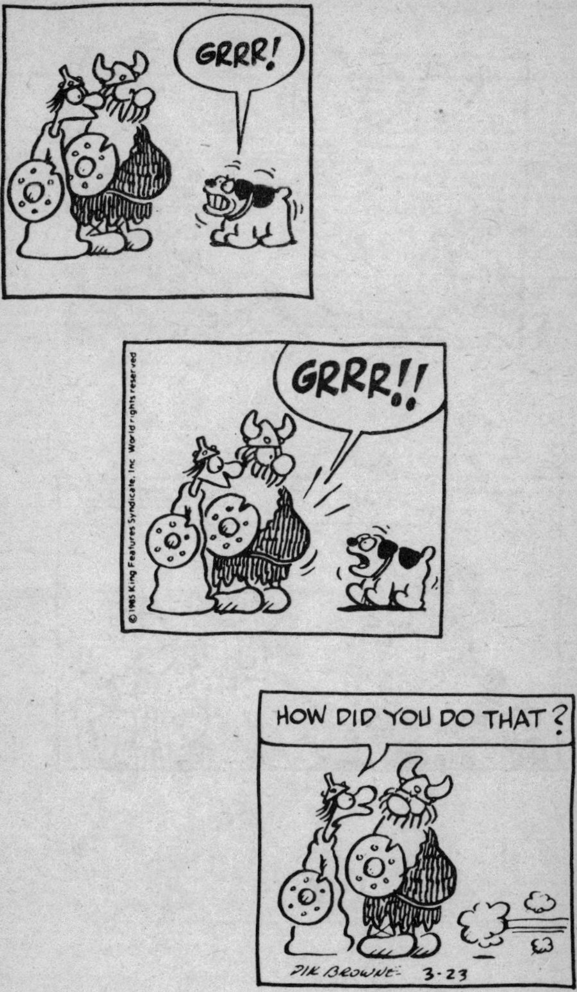
GRRR!
GRRR!!
© 1985 King Features Syndicate, Inc. World rights reserved
HOW DID YOU DO THAT?
DIK BROWNE 3-23

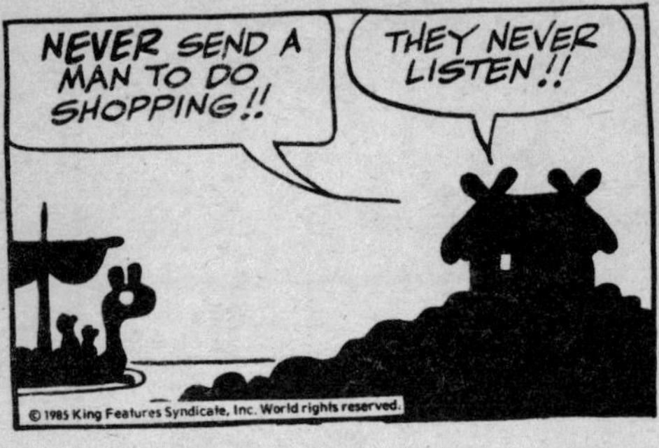
NEVER SEND A MAN TO DO SHOPPING!!
THEY NEVER LISTEN!!
© 1985 King Features Syndicate, Inc. World rights reserved.

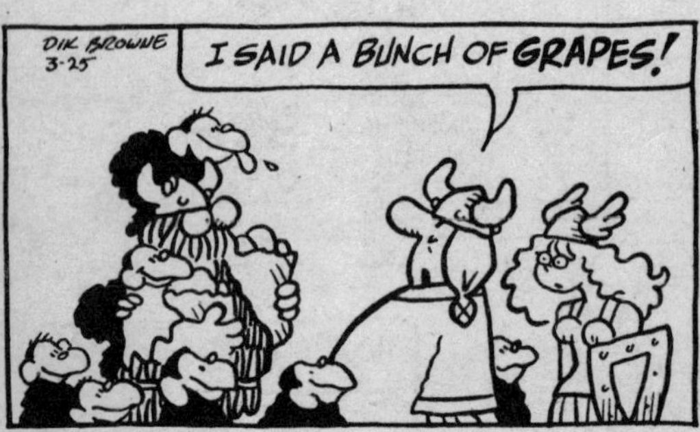
DIK BROWNE 3-25
I SAID A BUNCH OF GRAPES!

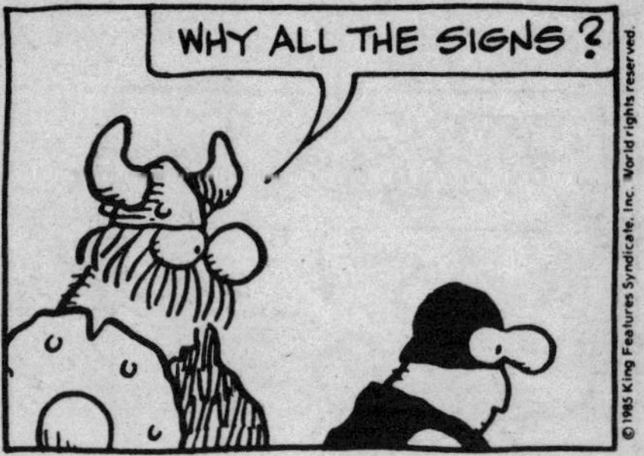
WHY ALL THE SIGNS?
© 1985 King Features Syndicate, Inc. World rights reserved.

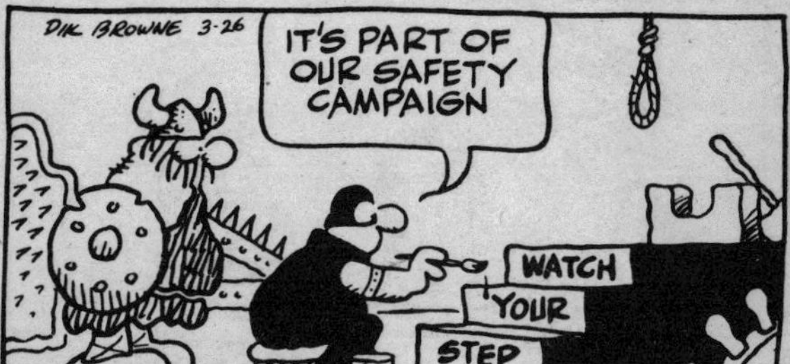
DIK BROWNE 3-26
IT'S PART OF OUR SAFETY CAMPAIGN
WATCH
YOUR
STEP

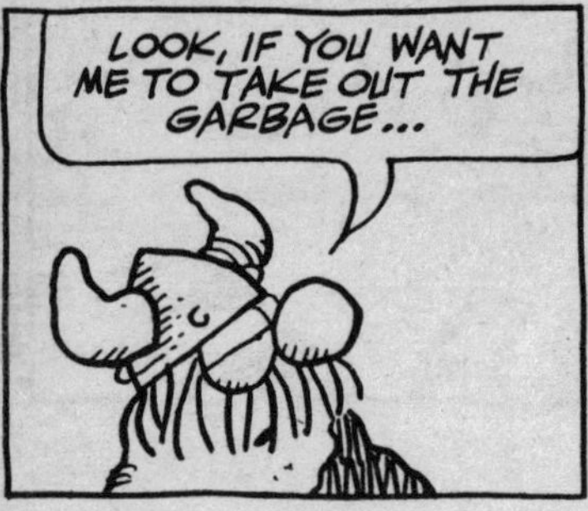
LOOK, IF YOU WANT ME TO TAKE OUT THE GARBAGE...

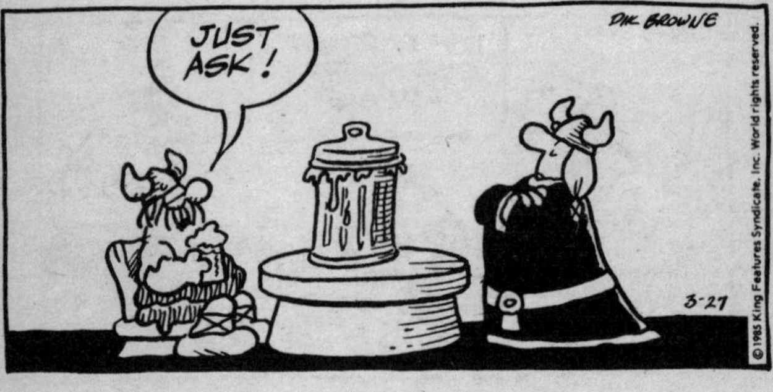
JUST ASK!
DIK BROWNE
3-27
© 1985 King Features Syndicate, Inc. World rights reserved.

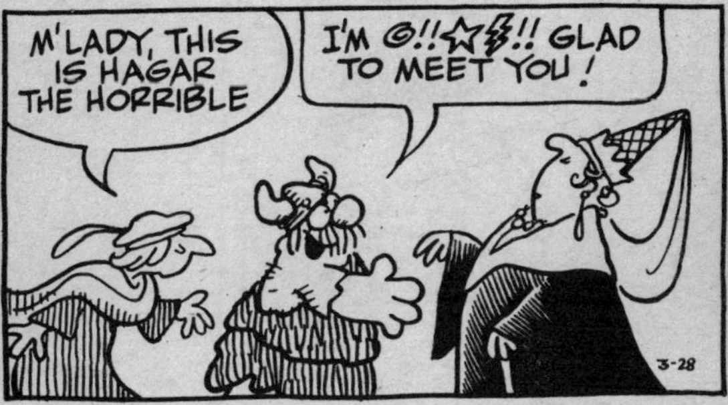
M'LADY, THIS IS HAGAR THE HORRIBLE
I'M @!!☆⚡!! GLAD TO MEET YOU!
3-28

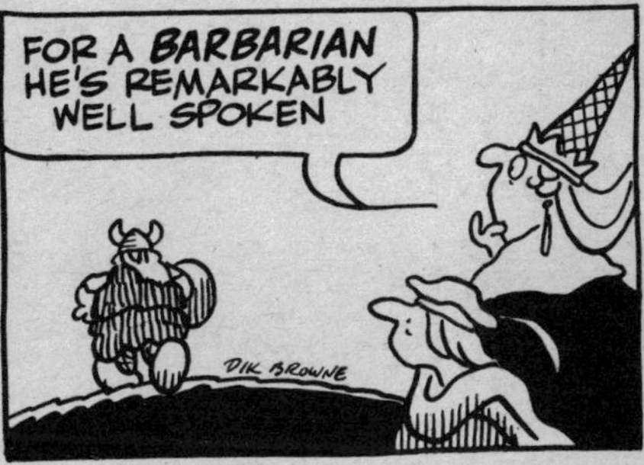
FOR A BARBARIAN HE'S REMARKABLY WELL SPOKEN
DIK BROWNE

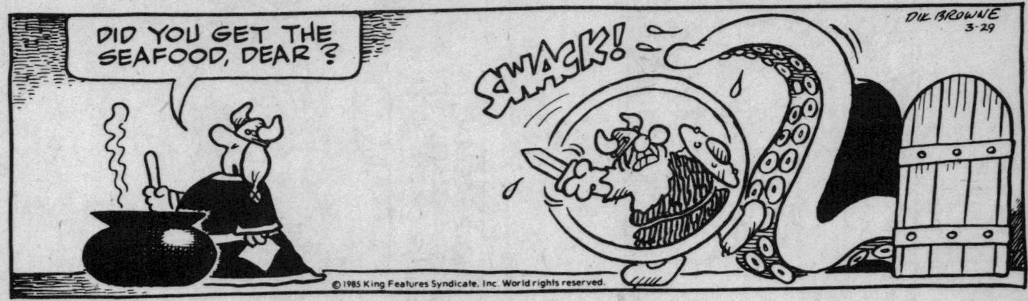
DID YOU GET THE SEAFOOD, DEAR ?
SWACK!
DIK BROWNE 3-29
© 1985 King Features Syndicate, Inc. World rights reserved.

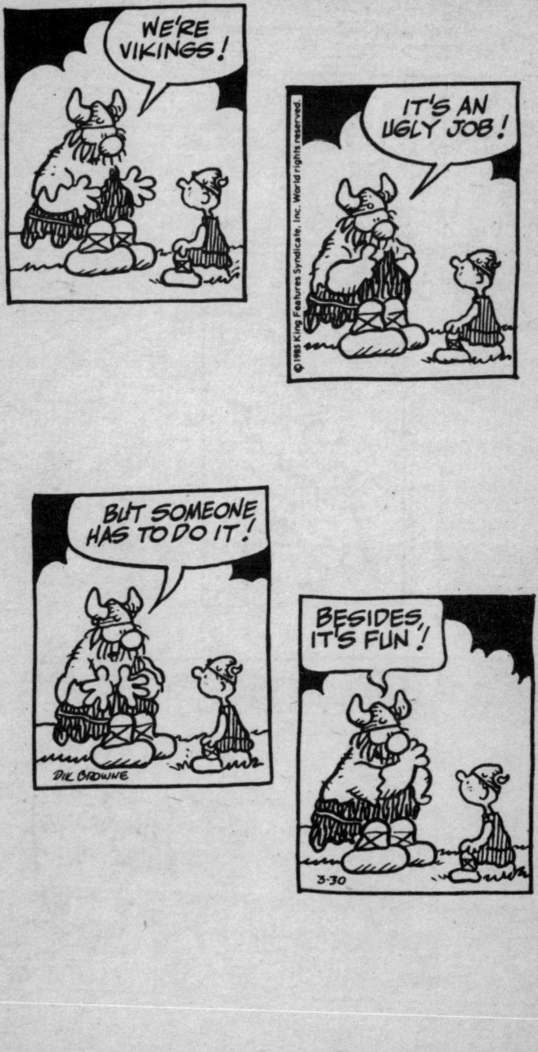
WE'RE VIKINGS!
IT'S AN UGLY JOB!
© 1985 King Features Syndicate, Inc. World rights reserved.
BUT SOMEONE HAS TO DO IT!
DIK BROWNE
BESIDES, IT'S FUN!
3-30

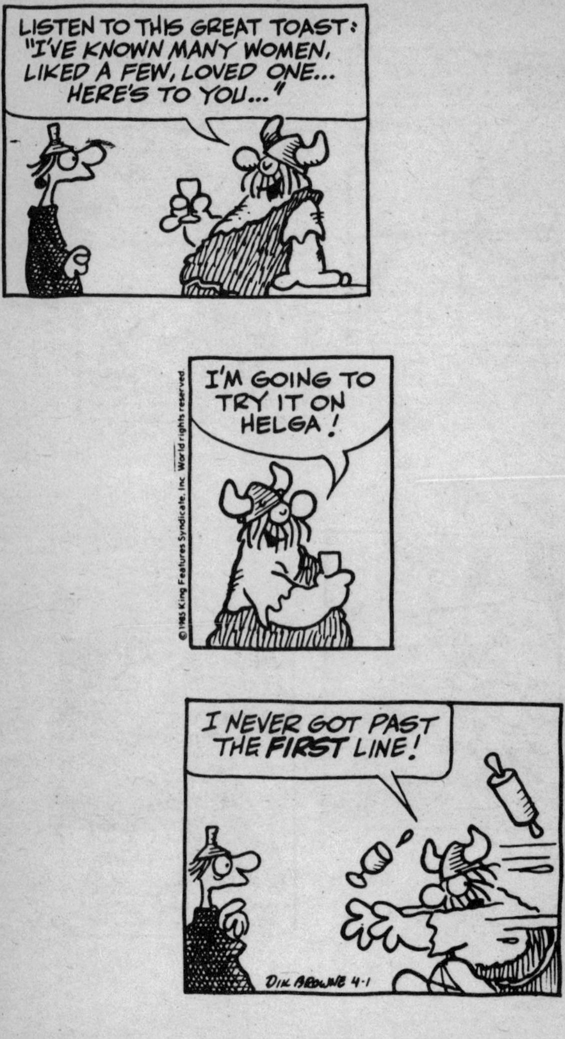
LISTEN TO THIS GREAT TOAST: "I'VE KNOWN MANY WOMEN, LIKED A FEW, LOVED ONE... HERE'S TO YOU..."
I'M GOING TO TRY IT ON HELGA!
I NEVER GOT PAST THE FIRST LINE!
DIK BROWNE 4-1

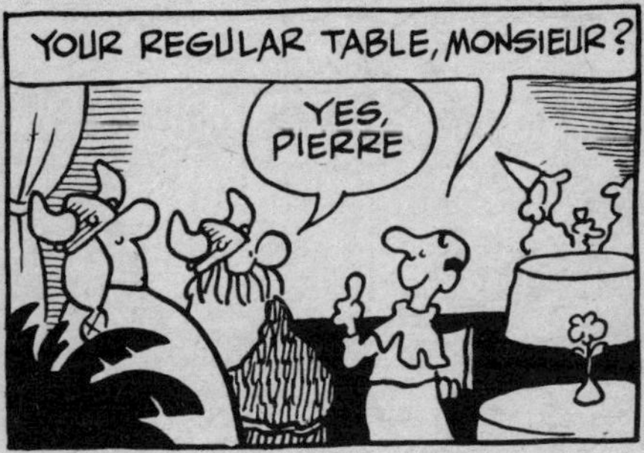
YOUR REGULAR TABLE, MONSIEUR?
YES, PIERRE

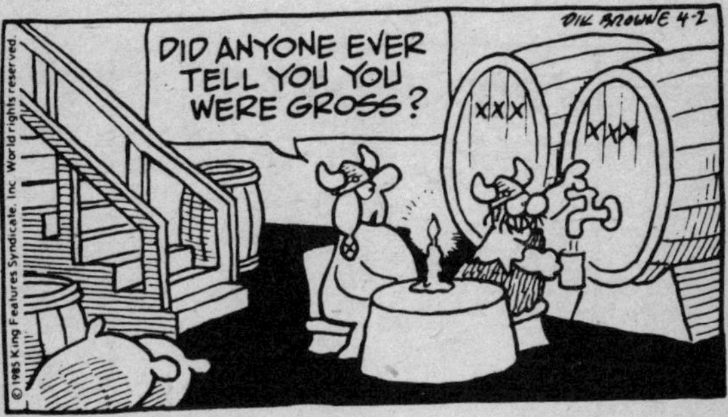
DIK BROWNE 4-2
DID ANYONE EVER TELL YOU YOU WERE GROSS?
© 1985 King Features Syndicate, Inc. World rights reserved.

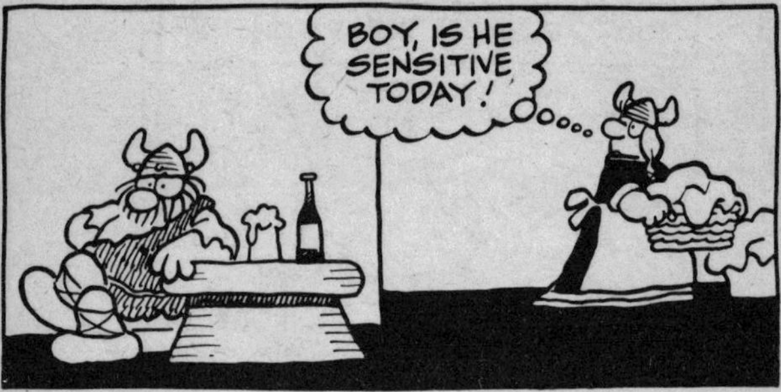
BOY, IS HE SENSITIVE TODAY!

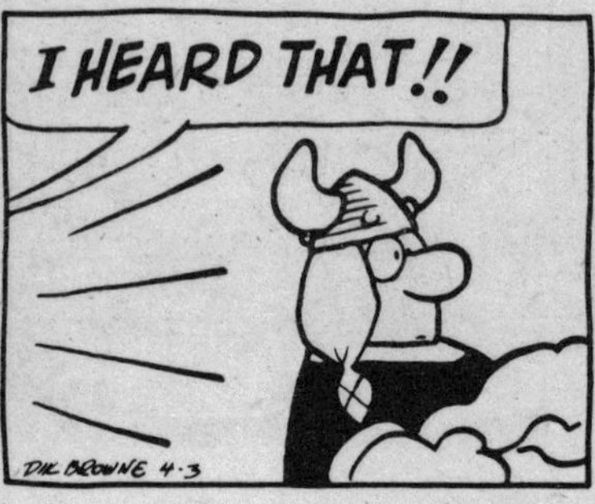
I HEARD THAT!!
DIK BROWNE 4-3

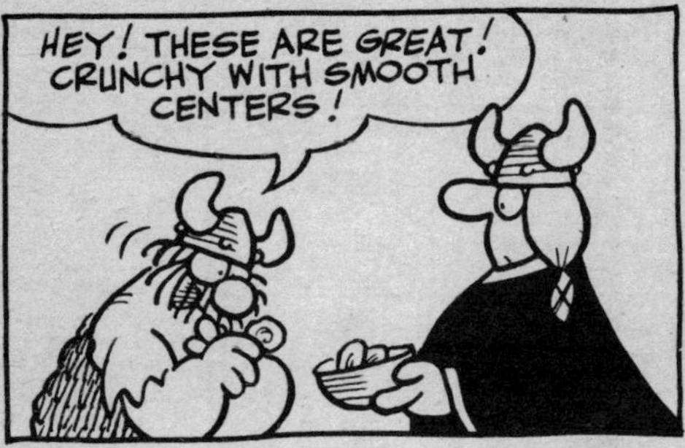
HEY! THESE ARE GREAT! CRUNCHY WITH SMOOTH CENTERS!

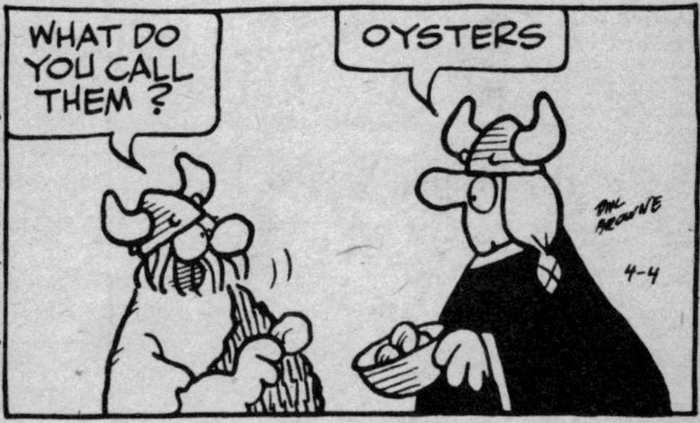
WHAT DO YOU CALL THEM?
OYSTERS
4-4

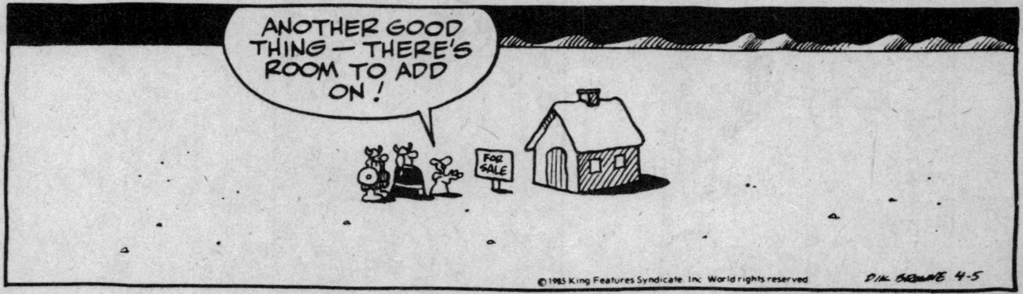
ANOTHER GOOD THING — THERE'S ROOM TO ADD ON!
FOR SALE
© 1985 King Features Syndicate, Inc. World rights reserved
DIK BROWNE 4-5

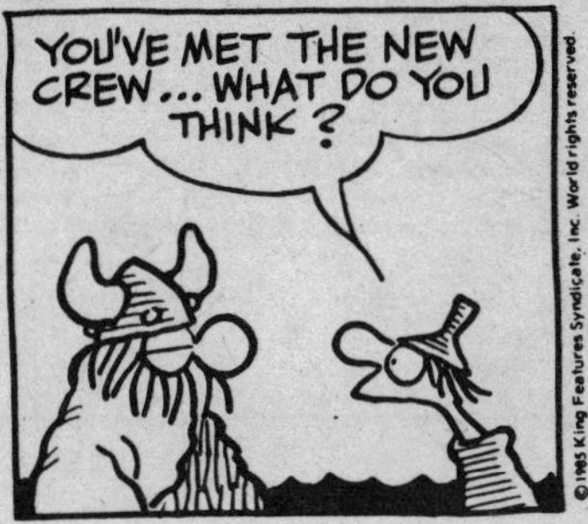
YOU'VE MET THE NEW CREW... WHAT DO YOU THINK?
© 1985 King Features Syndicate, Inc. World rights reserved.

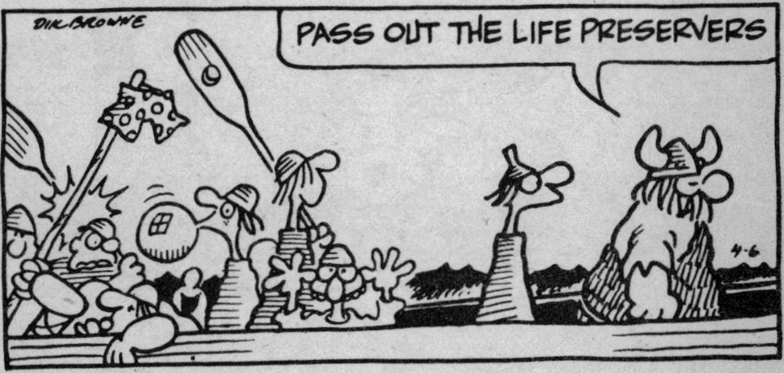
DIK BROWNE
PASS OUT THE LIFE PRESERVERS
4·6

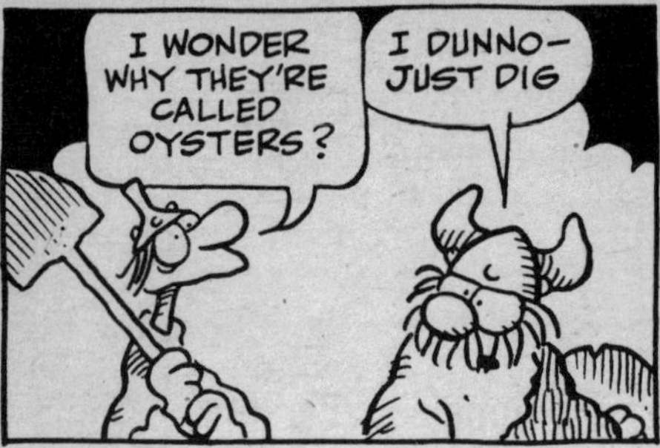
I WONDER WHY THEY'RE CALLED OYSTERS?
I DUNNO- JUST DIG

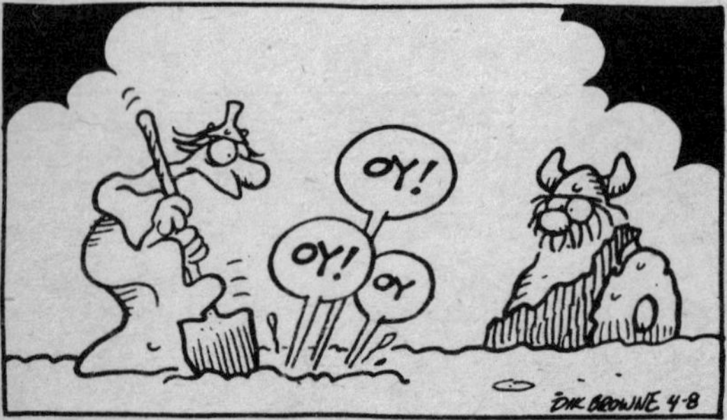
OY!
OY!
OY
DIK BROWNE 4-8

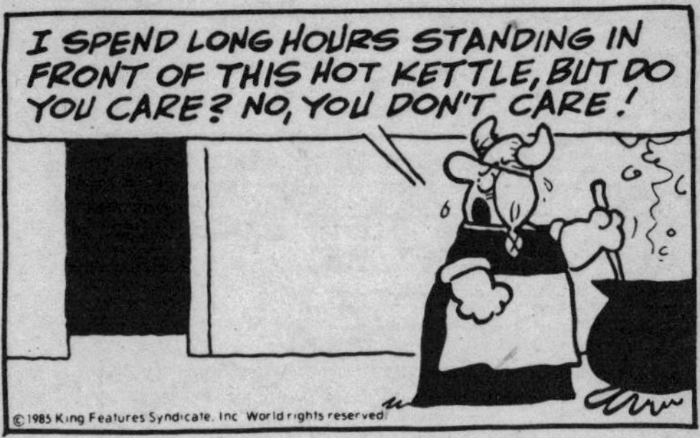
I SPEND LONG HOURS STANDING IN FRONT OF THIS HOT KETTLE, BUT DO YOU CARE? NO, YOU DON'T CARE!
© 1985 King Features Syndicate, Inc. World rights reserved.

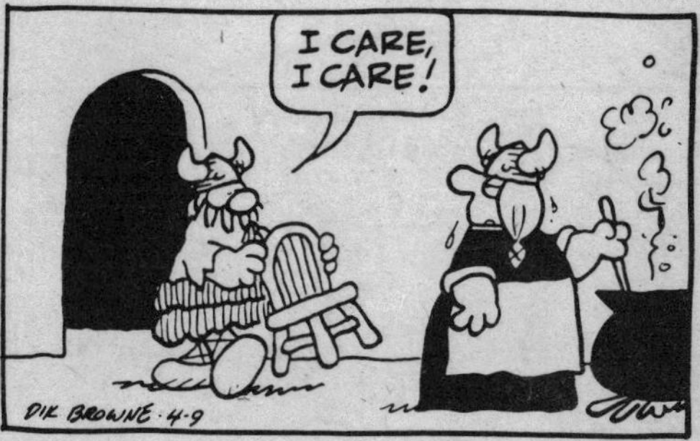
I CARE, I CARE!
DIK BROWNE · 4-9

THIS IS A BRILLIANT PLAN, HAGAR... THEY HAVE TO DUMP THEIR GARBAGE SOMETIME!
FRUMPITY FRUMP
FRUMP!
DIK BROWNE 4-10
© 1985 King Features Syndicate, Inc. World rights reserved

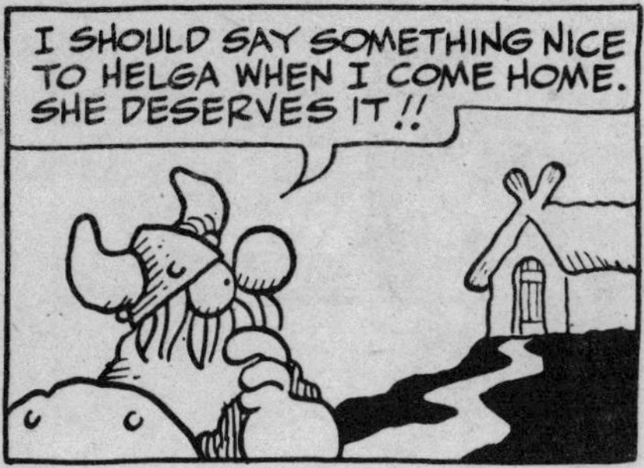
I SHOULD SAY SOMETHING NICE TO HELGA WHEN I COME HOME. SHE DESERVES IT!!

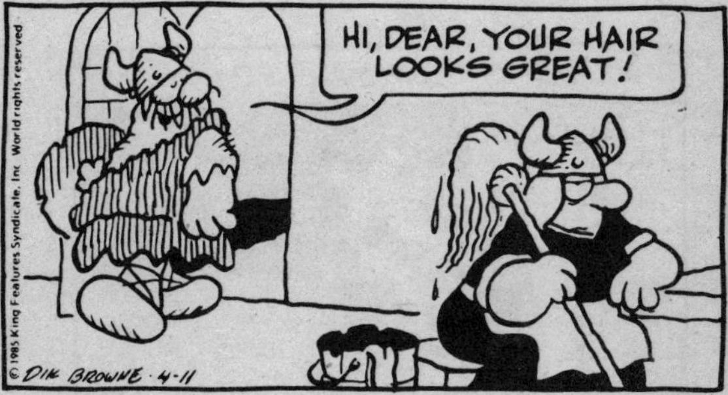
HI, DEAR, YOUR HAIR LOOKS GREAT!
© 1985 King Features Syndicate, Inc. World rights reserved
DIK BROWNE · 4-11

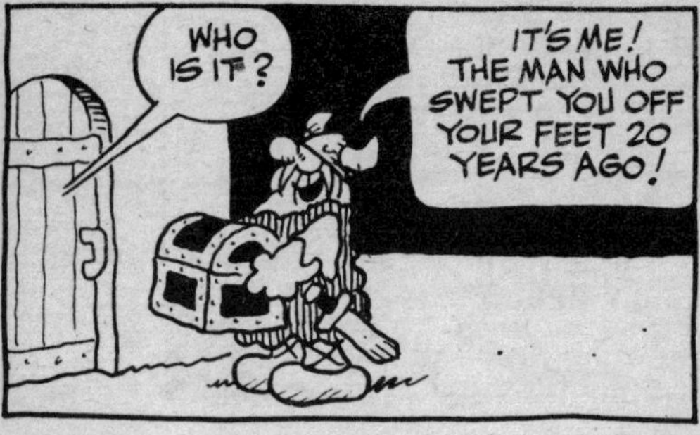
WHO IS IT?
IT'S ME! THE MAN WHO SWEPT YOU OFF YOUR FEET 20 YEARS AGO!

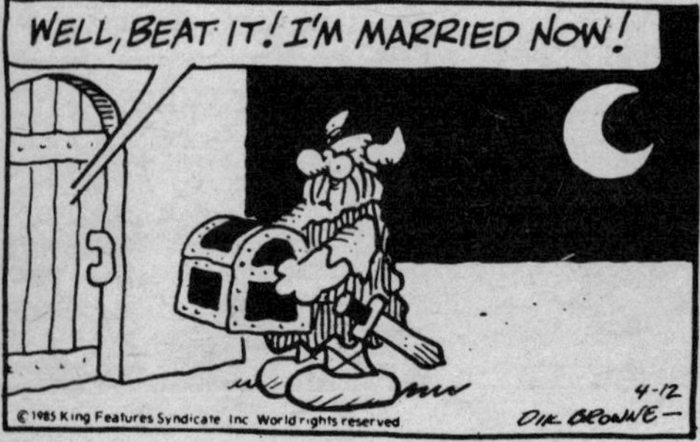
WELL, BEAT IT! I'M MARRIED NOW!
4-12
DIK BROWNE

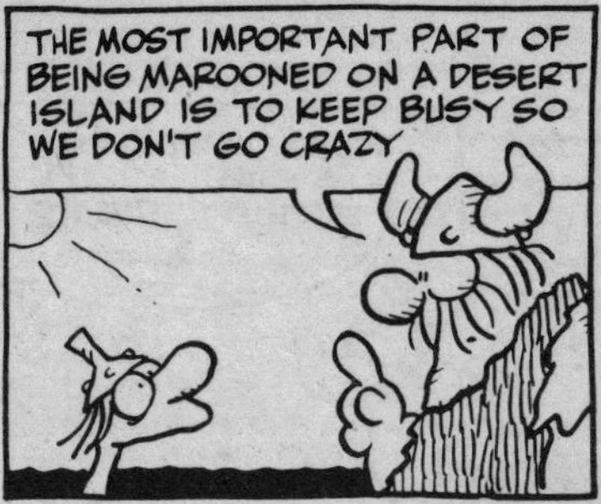
THE MOST IMPORTANT PART OF BEING MAROONED ON A DESERT ISLAND IS TO KEEP BUSY SO WE DON'T GO CRAZY

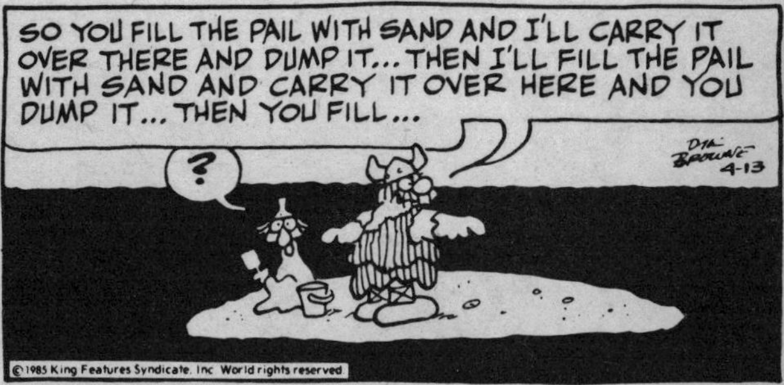
SO YOU FILL THE PAIL WITH SAND AND I'LL CARRY IT OVER THERE AND DUMP IT... THEN I'LL FILL THE PAIL WITH SAND AND CARRY IT OVER HERE AND YOU DUMP IT... THEN YOU FILL...
?
4-13
© 1985 King Features Syndicate, Inc. World rights reserved.

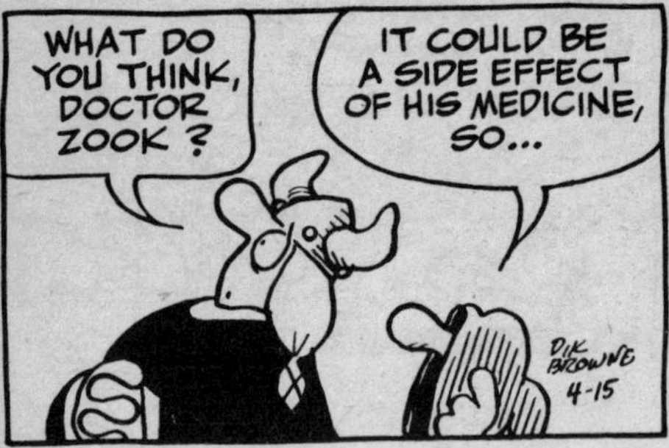
WHAT DO YOU THINK, DOCTOR ZOOK ?
IT COULD BE A SIDE EFFECT OF HIS MEDICINE, SO...
DIK BROWNE 4-15

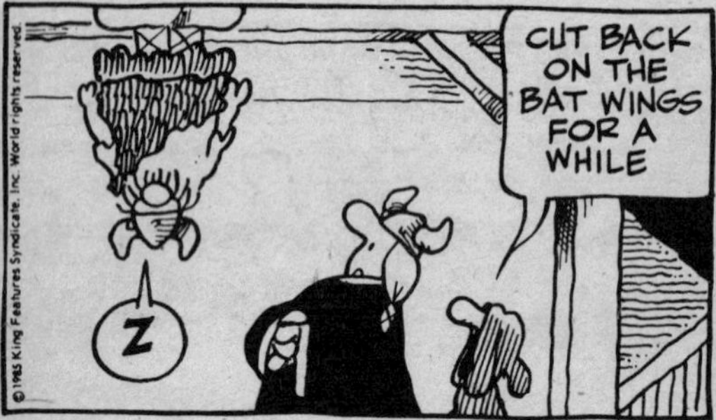
CUT BACK ON THE BAT WINGS FOR A WHILE
Z
© 1985 King Features Syndicate, Inc. World rights reserved.

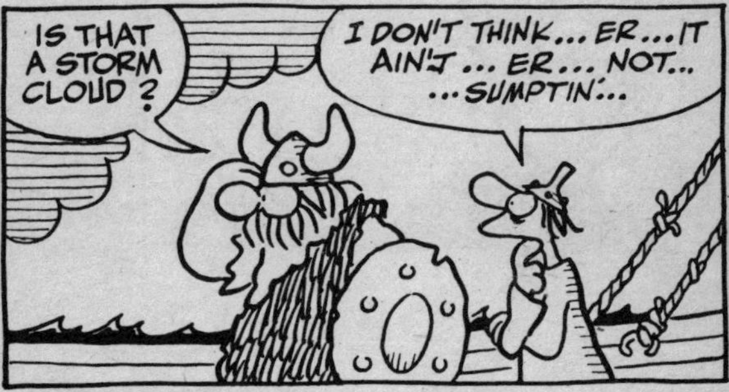
IS THAT A STORM CLOUD ?
I DON'T THINK... ER... IT AIN'T ... ER... NOT... ...SUMPTIN'...

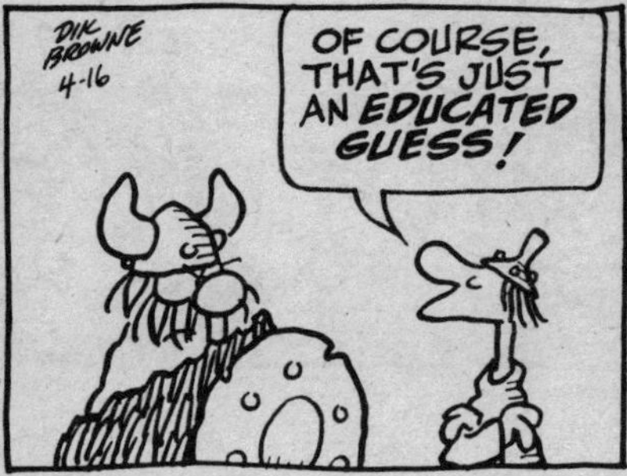
DIK BROWNE 4-16
OF COURSE, THAT'S JUST AN *EDUCATED GUESS!*

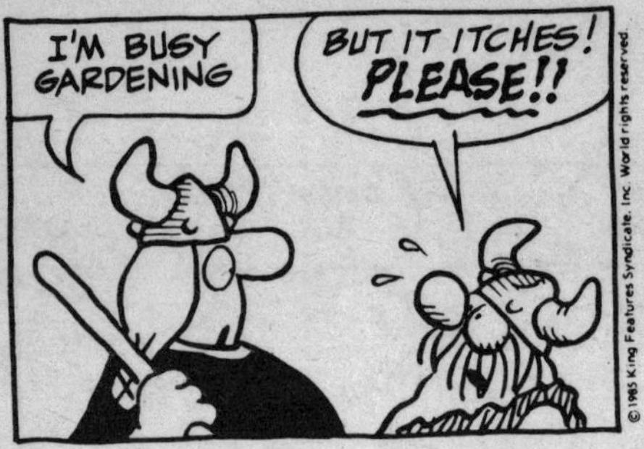
I'M BUSY GARDENING
BUT IT ITCHES! PLEASE!!
© 1985 King Features Syndicate, Inc. World rights reserved.

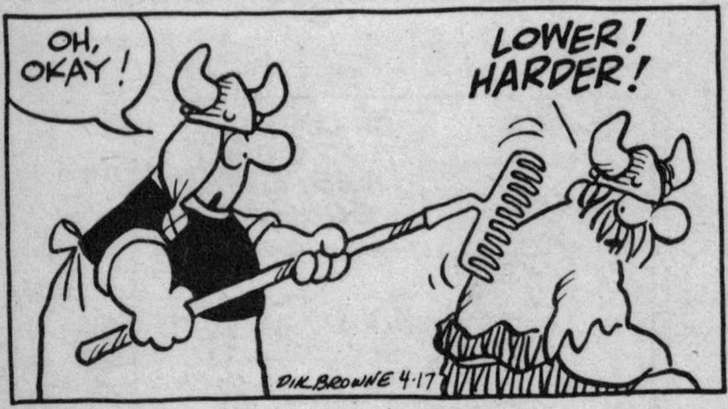
OH, OKAY!
LOWER! HARDER!
DIK BROWNE 4·17

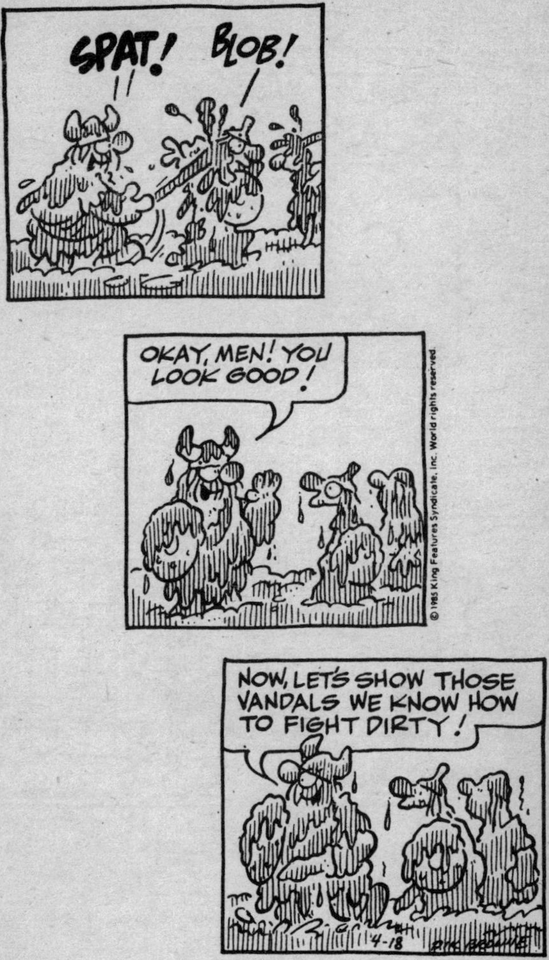
SPAT!
BLOB!
OKAY, MEN! YOU LOOK GOOD!
© 1985 King Features Syndicate, Inc. World rights reserved.
NOW, LET'S SHOW THOSE VANDALS WE KNOW HOW TO FIGHT DIRTY!
4-18
RIK BROWNE

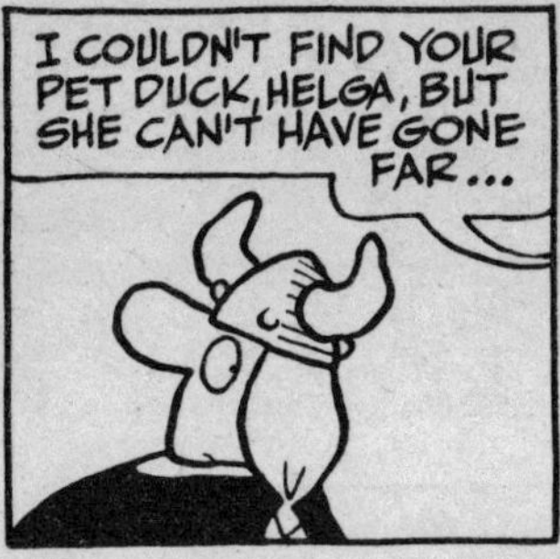
I COULDN'T FIND YOUR PET DUCK, HELGA, BUT SHE CAN'T HAVE GONE FAR...

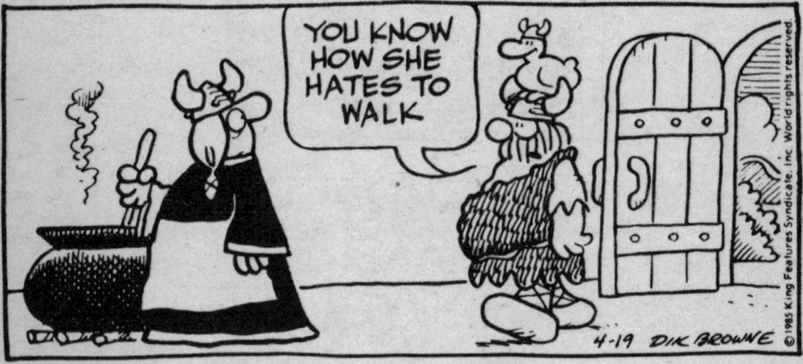
YOU KNOW HOW SHE HATES TO WALK
4-19 DIK BROWNE
© 1985 King Features Syndicate, Inc. World rights reserved.

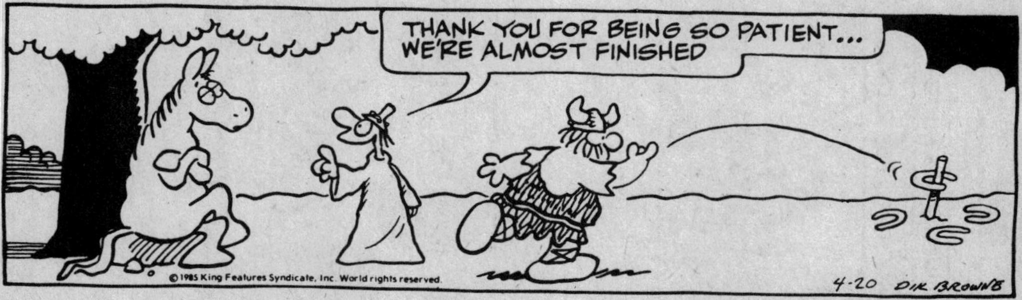
THANK YOU FOR BEING SO PATIENT... WE'RE ALMOST FINISHED
© 1985 King Features Syndicate, Inc. World rights reserved.
4-20 DIK BROWNE

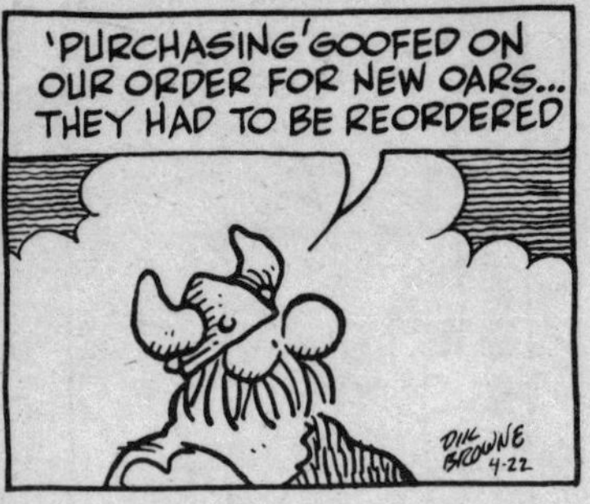
'PURCHASING' GOOFED ON OUR ORDER FOR NEW OARS... THEY HAD TO BE REORDERED
DIK BROWNE 4-22

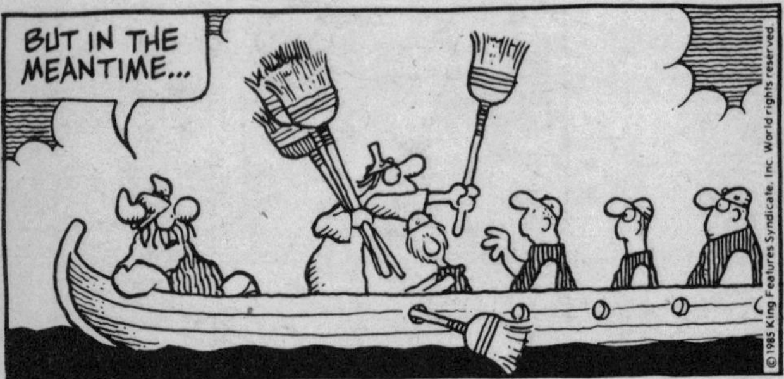
BUT IN THE MEANTIME...
© 1985 King Features Syndicate, Inc. World rights reserved.

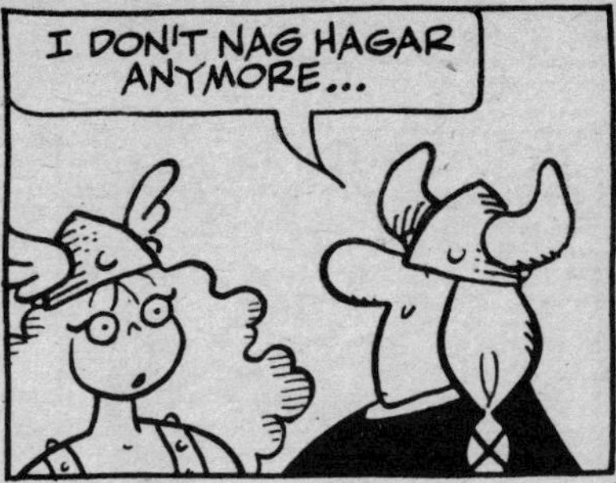
I DON'T NAG HAGAR ANYMORE...

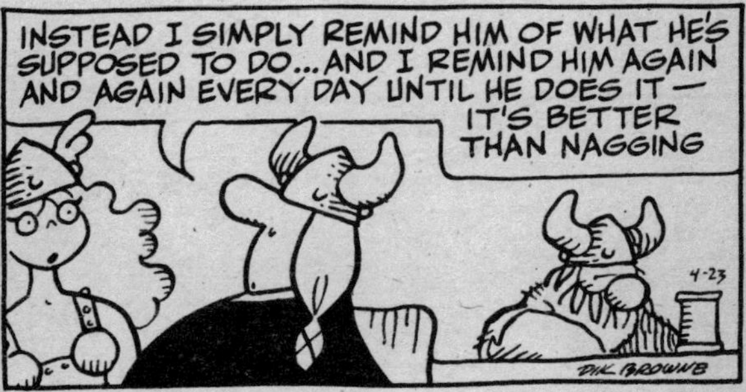
INSTEAD I SIMPLY REMIND HIM OF WHAT HE'S SUPPOSED TO DO...AND I REMIND HIM AGAIN AND AGAIN EVERY DAY UNTIL HE DOES IT— IT'S BETTER THAN NAGGING
4-23
DIK BROWNE

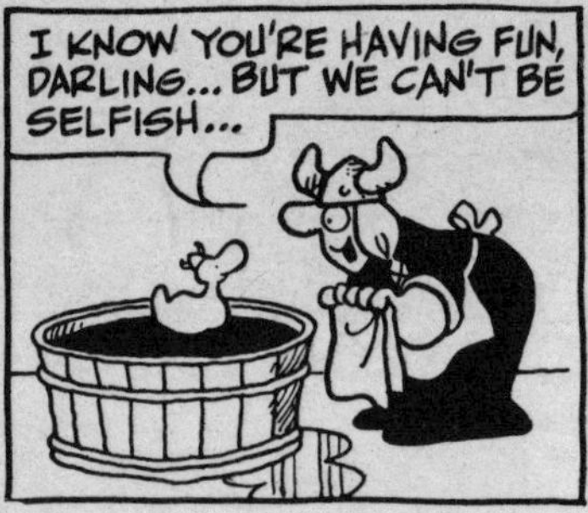
I KNOW YOU'RE HAVING FUN, DARLING... BUT WE CAN'T BE SELFISH...

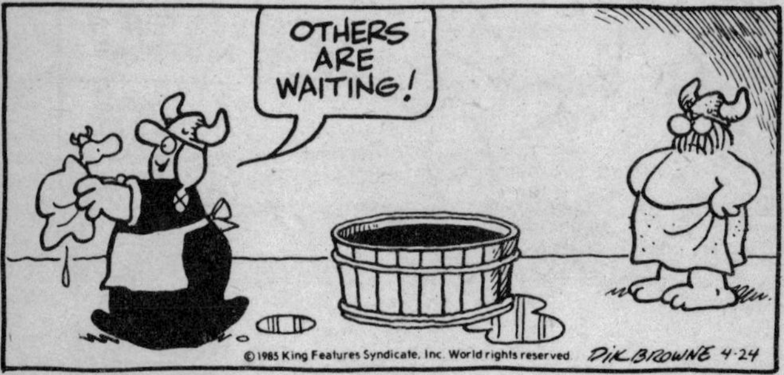
OTHERS ARE WAITING!
© 1985 King Features Syndicate, Inc. World rights reserved.
DIK BROWNE 4-24

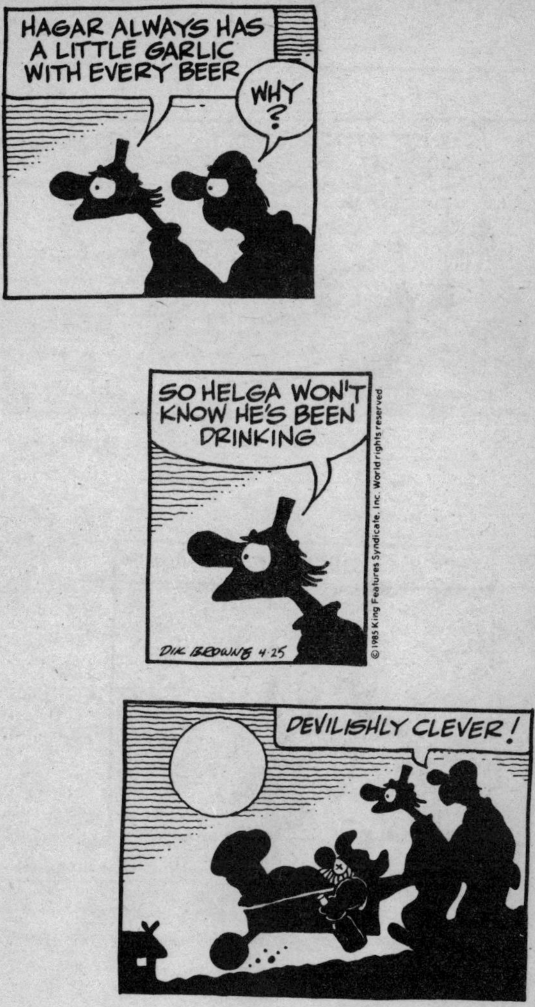
HAGAR ALWAYS HAS A LITTLE GARLIC WITH EVERY BEER
WHY ?
SO HELGA WON'T KNOW HE'S BEEN DRINKING
DIK BROWNE 4·25
DEVILISHLY CLEVER !

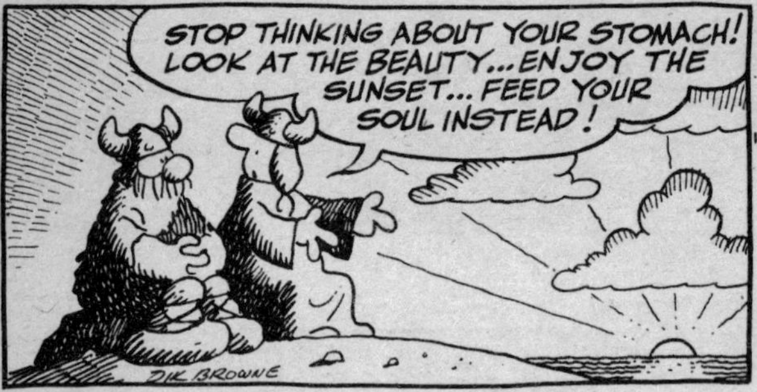
STOP THINKING ABOUT YOUR STOMACH! LOOK AT THE BEAUTY...ENJOY THE SUNSET...FEED YOUR SOUL INSTEAD!
DIK BROWNE

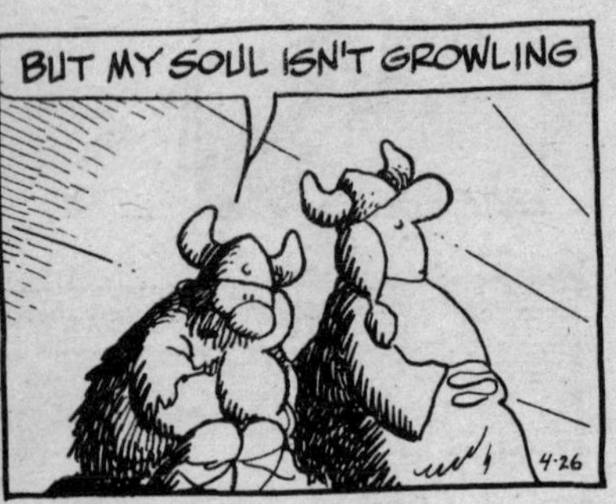
BUT MY SOUL ISN'T GROWLING
4·26

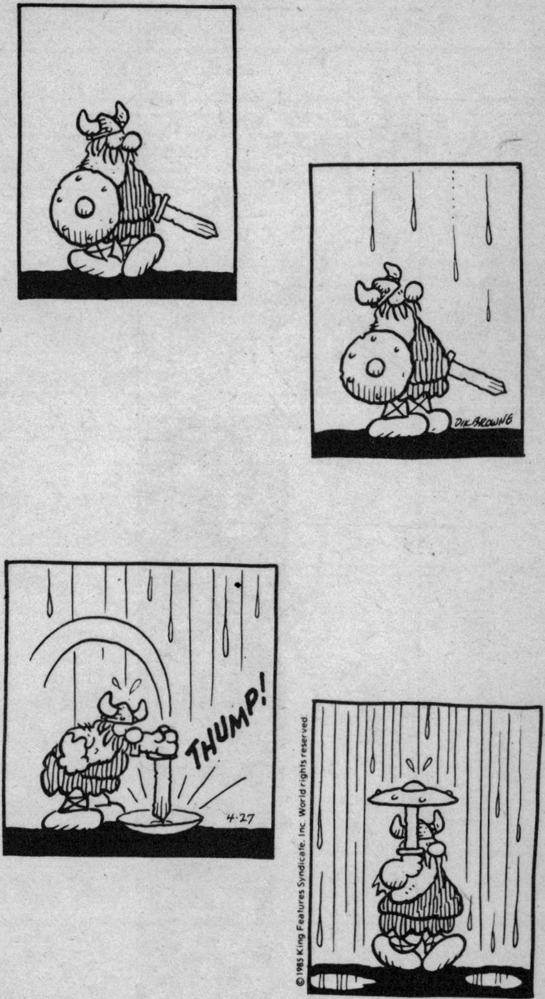
DIK BROWNE
THUMP!
4·27

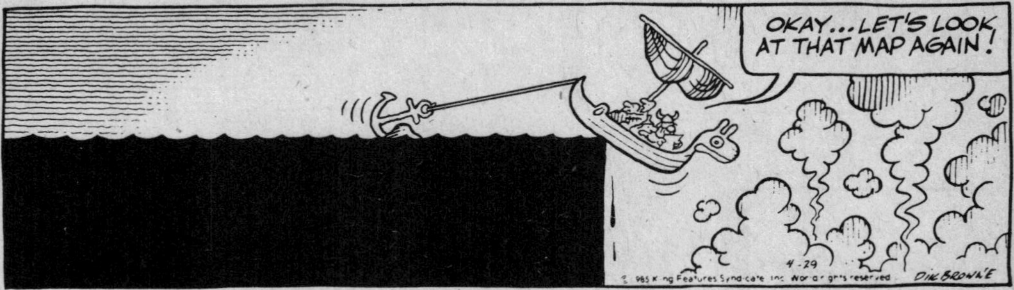
OKAY...LET'S LOOK AT THAT MAP AGAIN!
4-29
DIK BROWNE

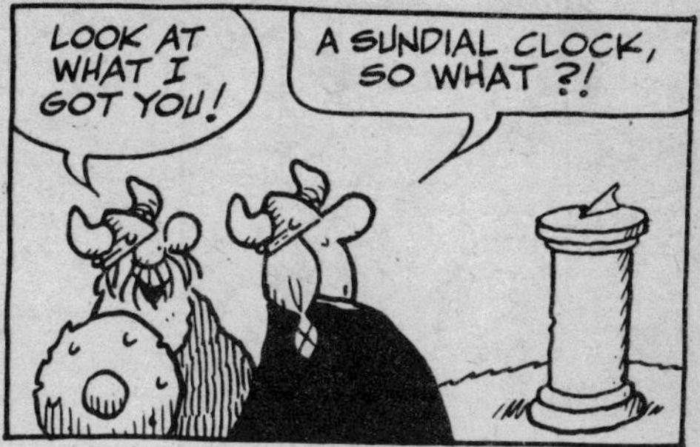
LOOK AT WHAT I GOT YOU!
A SUNDIAL CLOCK, SO WHAT ?!

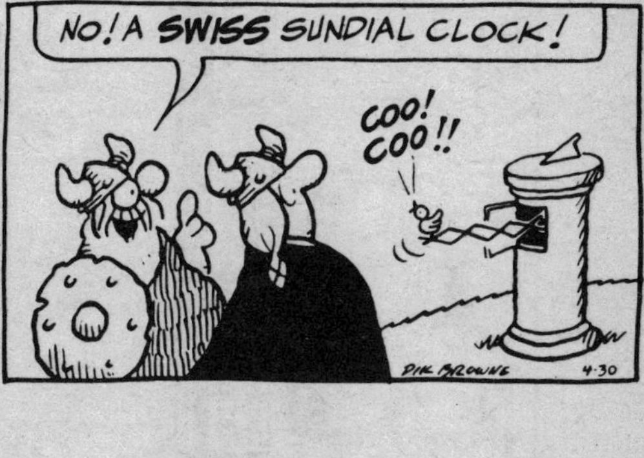
NO! A **SWISS** SUNDIAL CLOCK!
COO! COO!!
DIK BROWNE
4-30

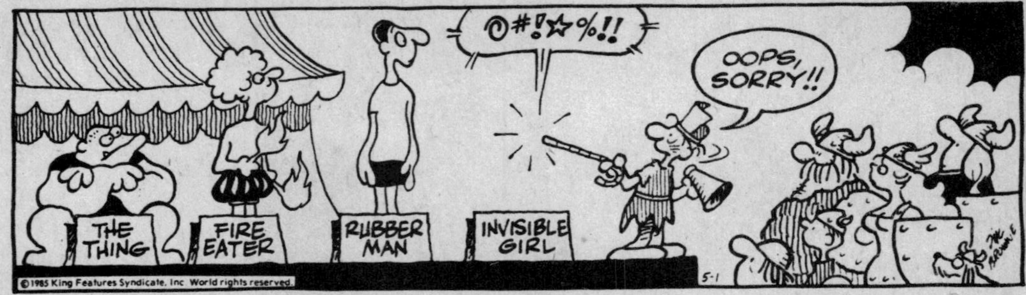
THE THING
FIRE EATER
RUBBER MAN
INVISIBLE GIRL
@#!☆%!!
OOPS, SORRY!!
5-1
© 1985 King Features Syndicate, Inc. World rights reserved.

WHEN YOU FIRST MET DADDY, WAS IT LOVE AT FIRST SIGHT?
THE FIRST TIME YOUR FATHER SAW ME HE FOLLOWED ME HOME LIKE A PUPPY DOG!
OF COURSE, SHE WAS CARRYING A BASKET OF FRIED CHICKEN AT THE TIME...
DIK BROWNE
5-2
© 1985 King Features Syndicate, Inc. World rights reserved

WHISKEY
WATER?
NO...
NO ADDITIVES!
DIK BROWNE
5·3

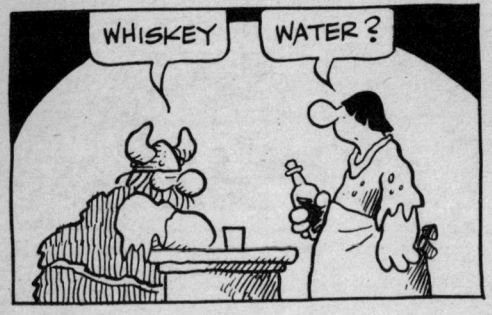

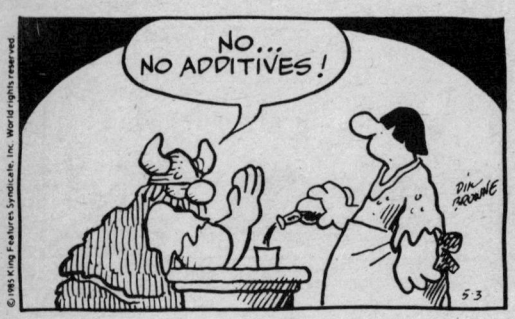

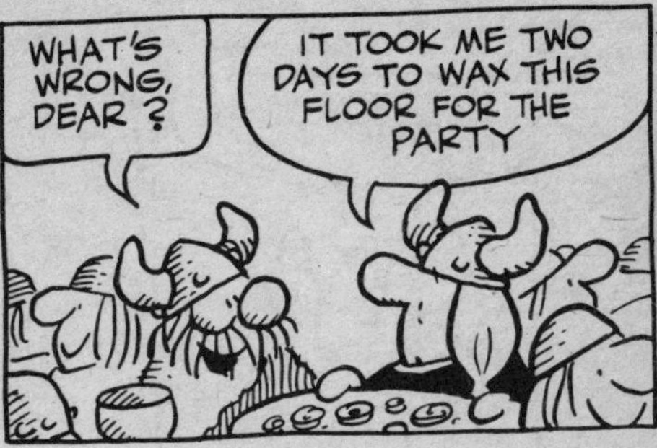
WHAT'S WRONG, DEAR ?
IT TOOK ME TWO DAYS TO WAX THIS FLOOR FOR THE PARTY

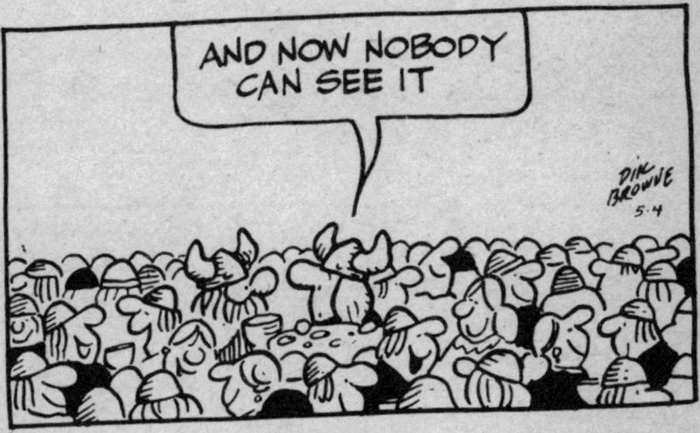
AND NOW NOBODY CAN SEE IT
DIK BROWNE
5·4

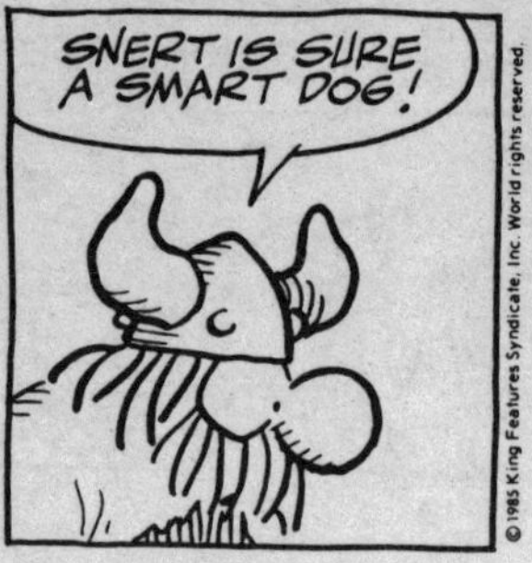
SNERT IS SURE A SMART DOG!
© 1985 King Features Syndicate, Inc. World rights reserved.

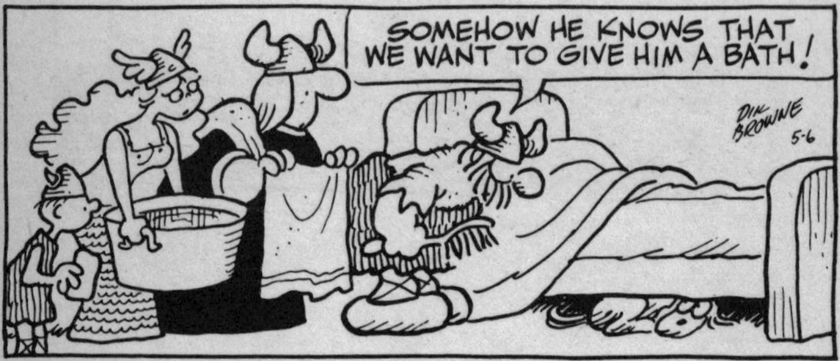
SOMEHOW HE KNOWS THAT WE WANT TO GIVE HIM A BATH!
DIK BROWNE
5-6

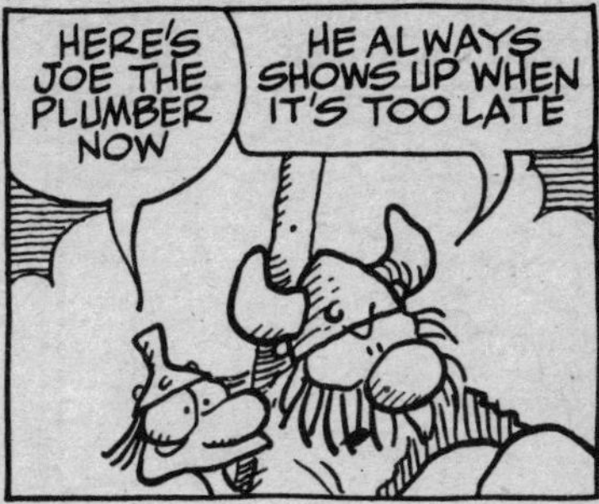
HERE'S JOE THE PLUMBER NOW
HE ALWAYS SHOWS UP WHEN IT'S TOO LATE

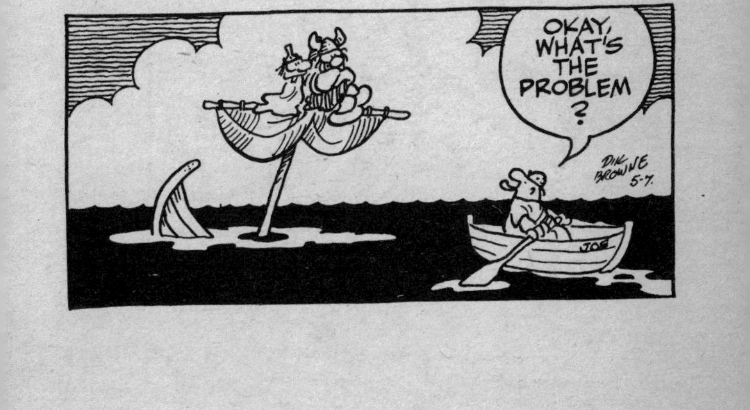
OKAY, WHAT'S THE PROBLEM ?
JOE
DIK BROWNE 5-7.

I'LL HAVE A CHILD'S PORTION
HEY!
DIK BROWNE 5-8

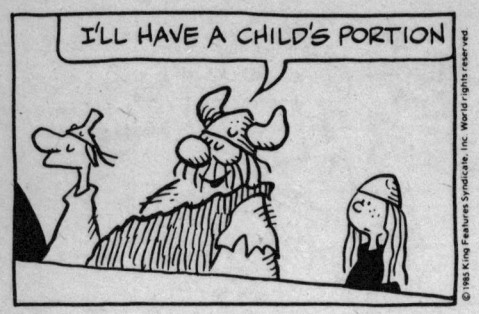

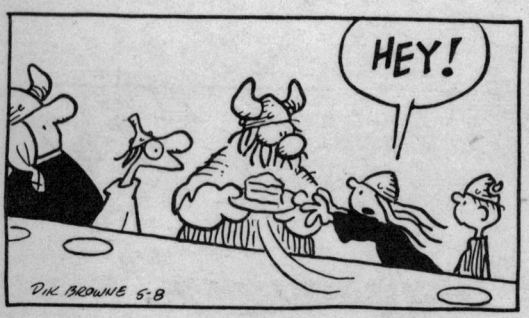

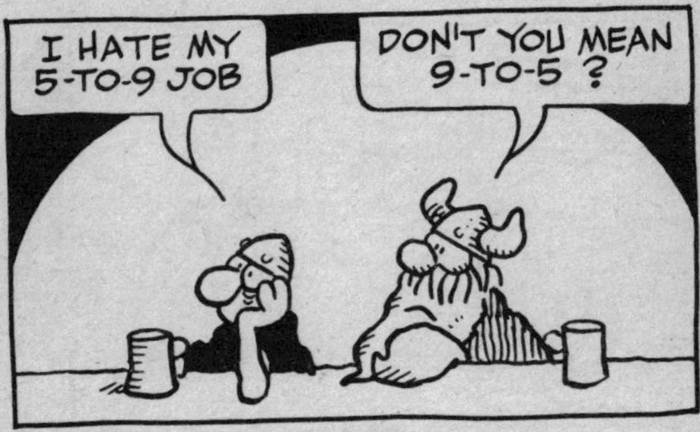
I HATE MY 5-TO-9 JOB
DON'T YOU MEAN 9-TO-5 ?

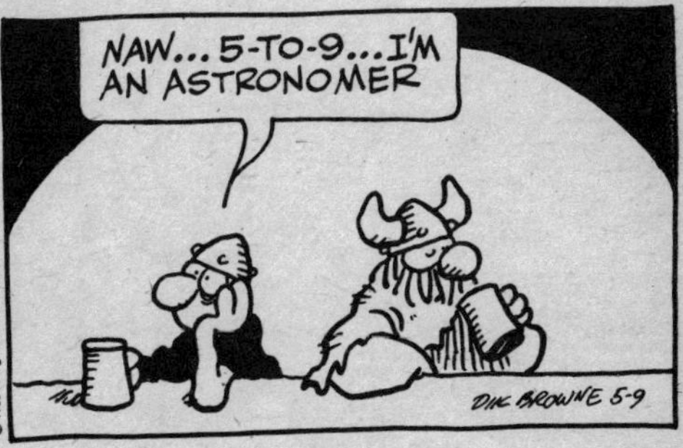
NAW... 5-TO-9... I'M AN ASTRONOMER
DIK BROWNE 5-9

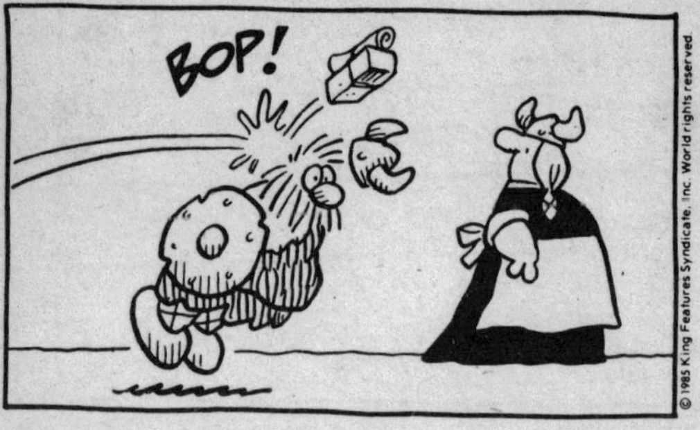
BOP!
© 1985 King Features Syndicate, Inc. World rights reserved.

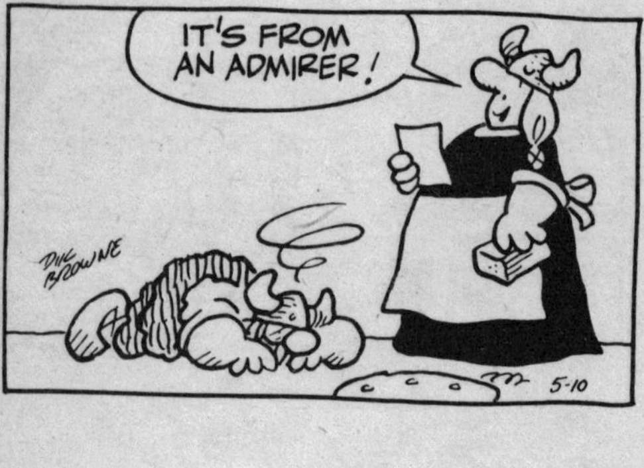
IT'S FROM AN ADMIRER!
DIK BROWNE
5-10

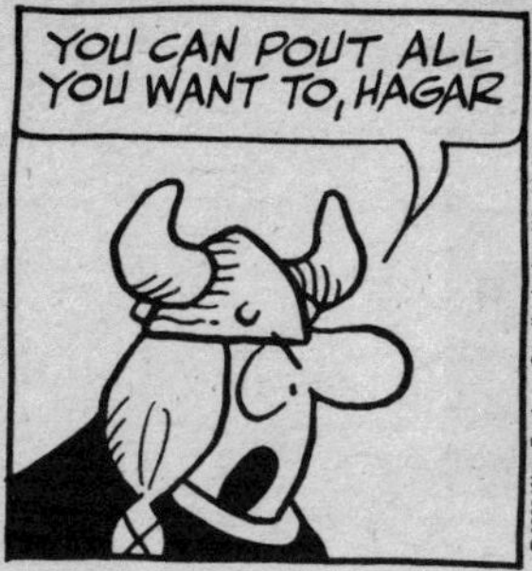
YOU CAN POUT ALL YOU WANT TO, HAGAR

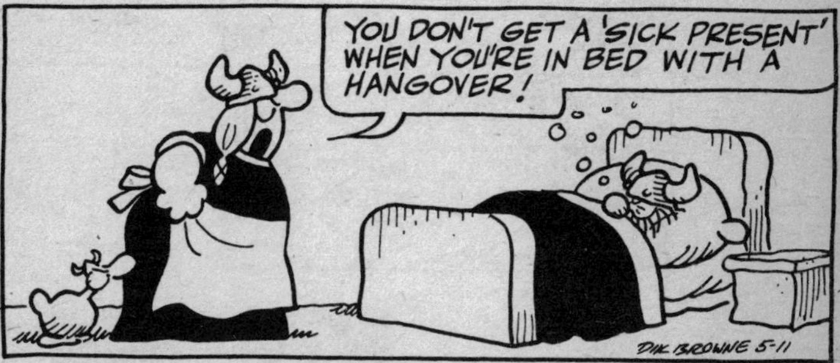
YOU DON'T GET A 'SICK PRESENT' WHEN YOU'RE IN BED WITH A HANGOVER!
DIK BROWNE 5-11

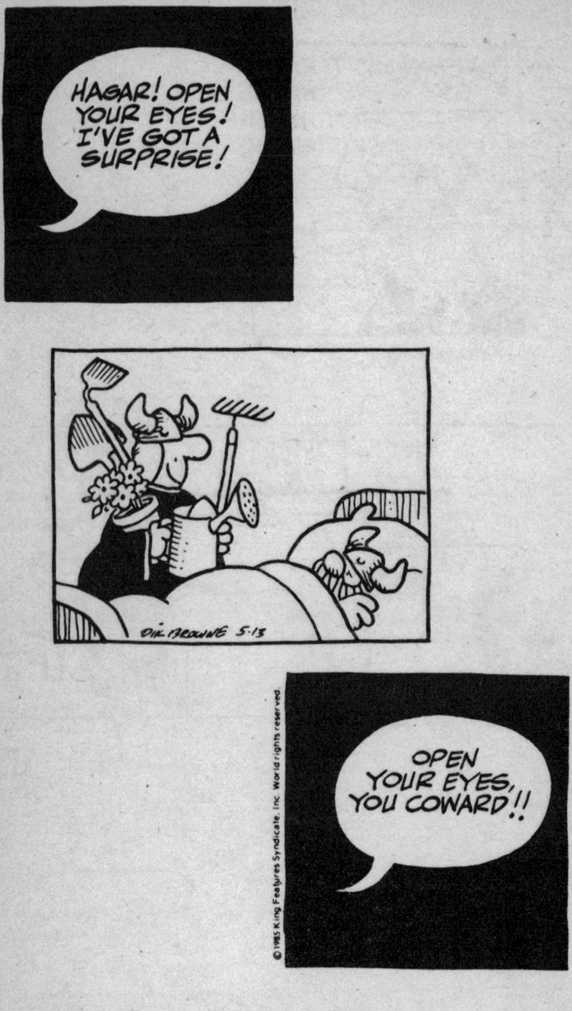
HAGAR! OPEN YOUR EYES! I'VE GOT A SURPRISE!
DIK BROWNE 5-13
OPEN YOUR EYES, YOU COWARD!!

WE JOKE ABOUT THE TAX COLLECTOR A LOT BUT HE'S REALLY A NICE GUY WHO'S JUST DOING HIS JOB AND WOULDN'T HURT A SOUL !!
© 1985 King Features Syndicate, Inc. World rights reserved.
SAY IT LOUDER–I DON'T THINK HE HEARD YOU !!
5-14 DIK BROWNE

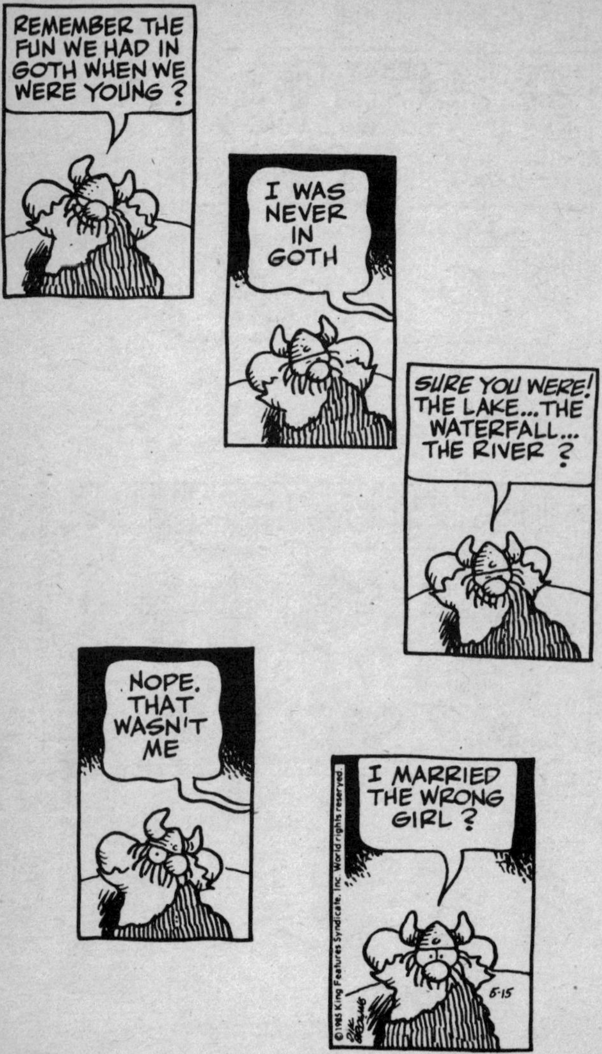
REMEMBER THE FUN WE HAD IN GOTH WHEN WE WERE YOUNG?
I WAS NEVER IN GOTH
SURE YOU WERE! THE LAKE...THE WATERFALL... THE RIVER?
NOPE. THAT WASN'T ME
I MARRIED THE WRONG GIRL?
©1985 King Features Syndicate, Inc. World rights reserved.
5-15

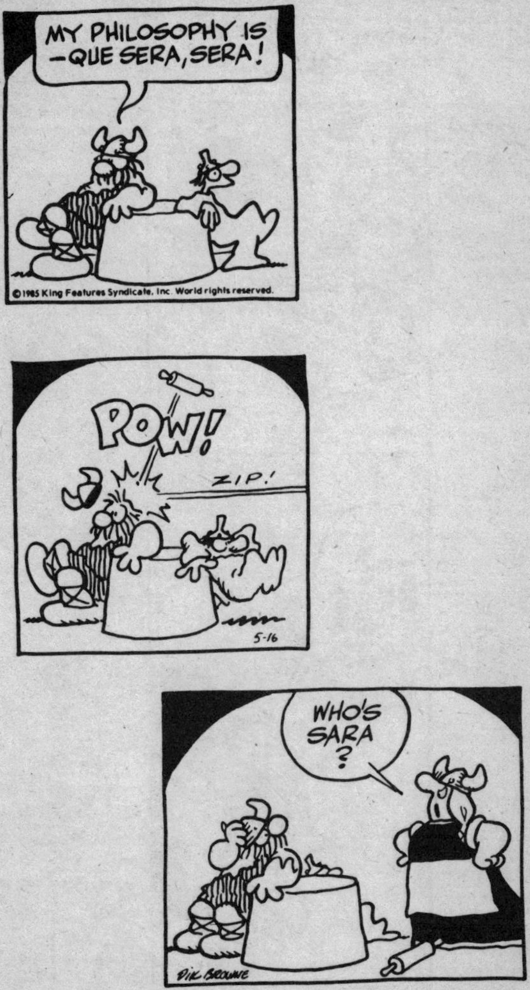
MY PHILOSOPHY IS —QUE SERA, SERA!
©1985 King Features Syndicate, Inc. World rights reserved.
POW!
ZIP!
5-16
WHO'S SARA ?
DIK BROWNE

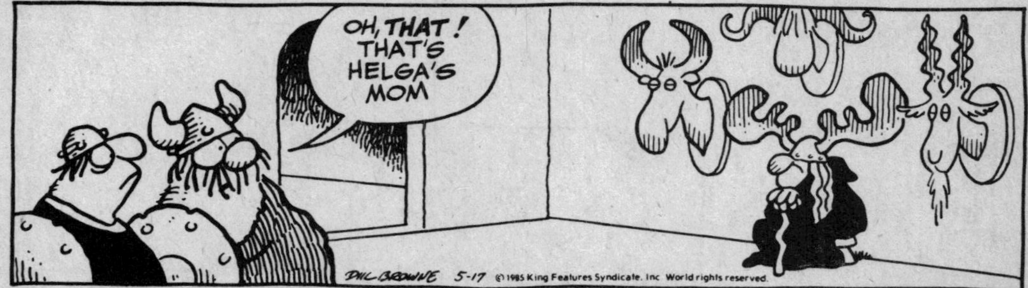
OH, THAT! THAT'S HELGA'S MOM
DIK BROWNE 5-17
© 1985 King Features Syndicate, Inc World rights reserved.

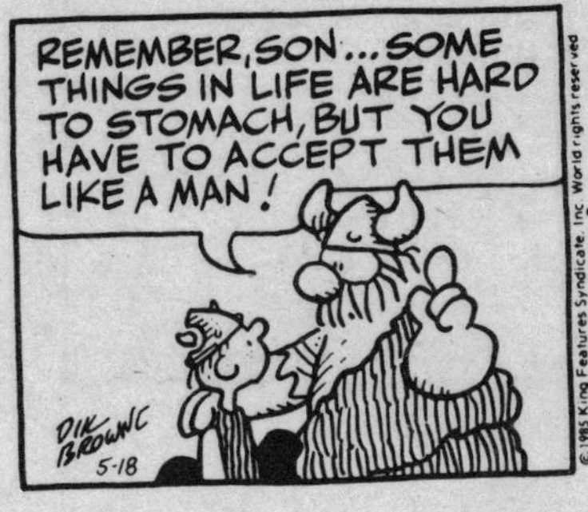
REMEMBER, SON... SOME THINGS IN LIFE ARE HARD TO STOMACH, BUT YOU HAVE TO ACCEPT THEM LIKE A MAN!
DIK BROWNE
5-18
© 1985 King Features Syndicate, Inc. World rights reserved

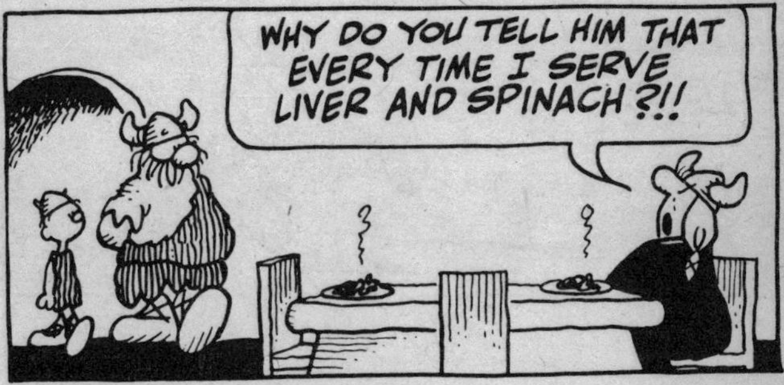
WHY DO YOU TELL HIM THAT EVERY TIME I SERVE LIVER AND SPINACH ?!!

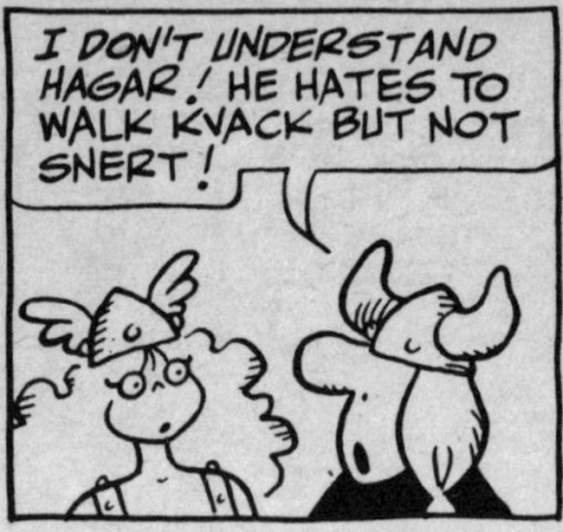
I DON'T UNDERSTAND HAGAR! HE HATES TO WALK KVACK BUT NOT SNERT!

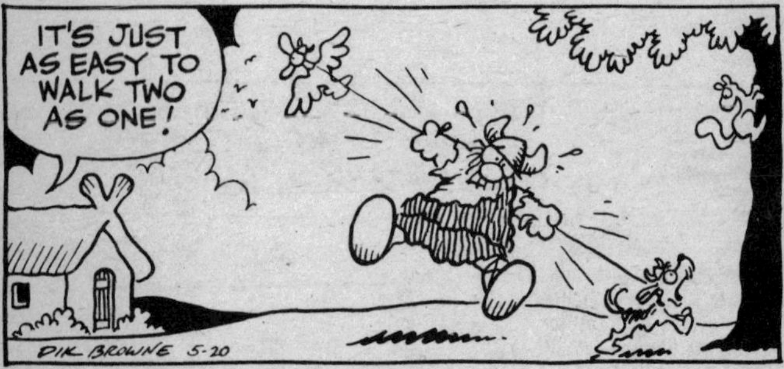
IT'S JUST AS EASY TO WALK TWO AS ONE!
DIK BROWNE 5-20

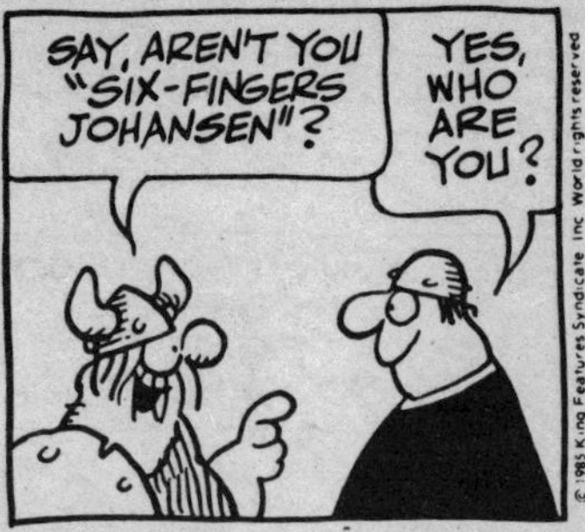
SAY, AREN'T YOU "SIX-FINGERS JOHANSEN"?
YES, WHO ARE YOU?
© 1985 King Features Syndicate Inc World rights reserved

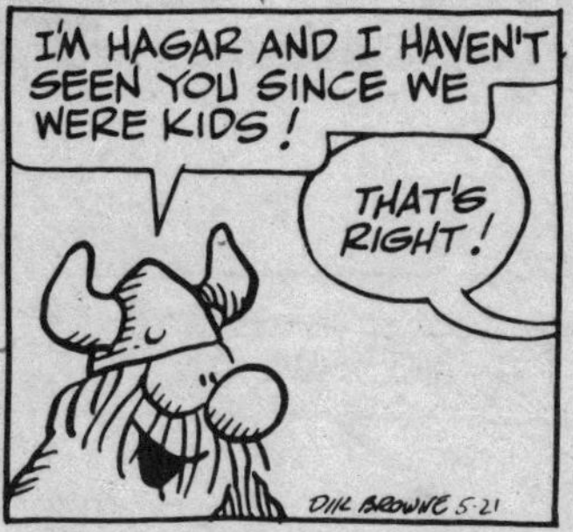
I'M HAGAR AND I HAVEN'T SEEN YOU SINCE WE WERE KIDS!
THAT'S RIGHT!
DIK BROWNE 5-21

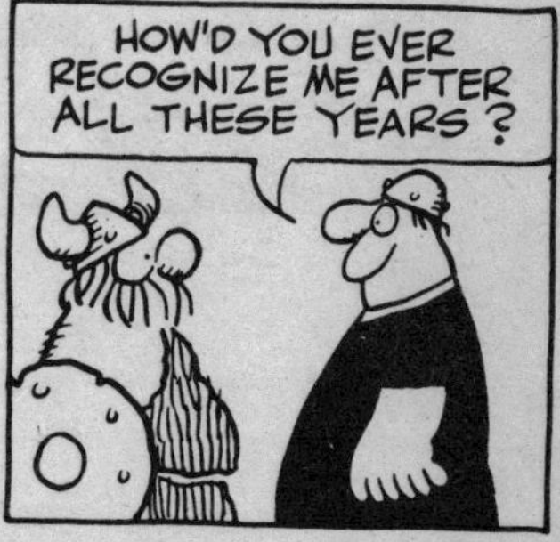
HOW'D YOU EVER RECOGNIZE ME AFTER ALL THESE YEARS?

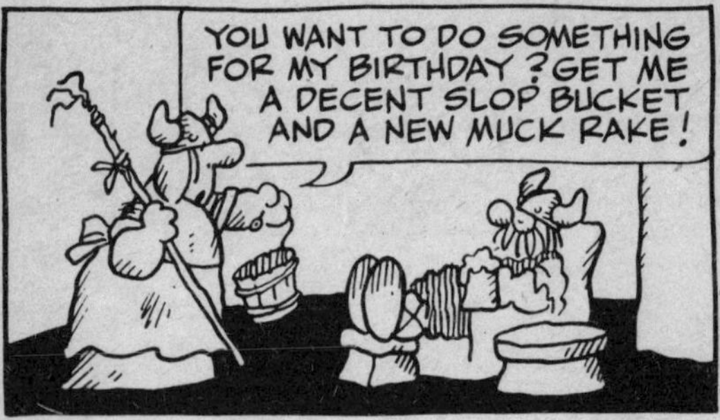
YOU WANT TO DO SOMETHING FOR MY BIRTHDAY ? GET ME A DECENT SLOP BUCKET AND A NEW MUCK RAKE !

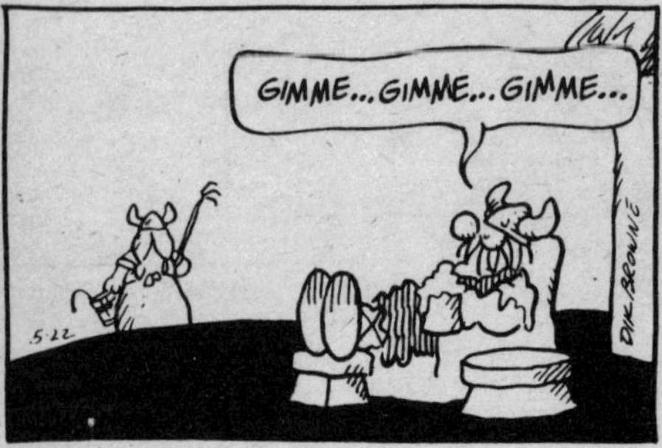
GIMME...GIMME...GIMME...
5·22
DIK BROWNE

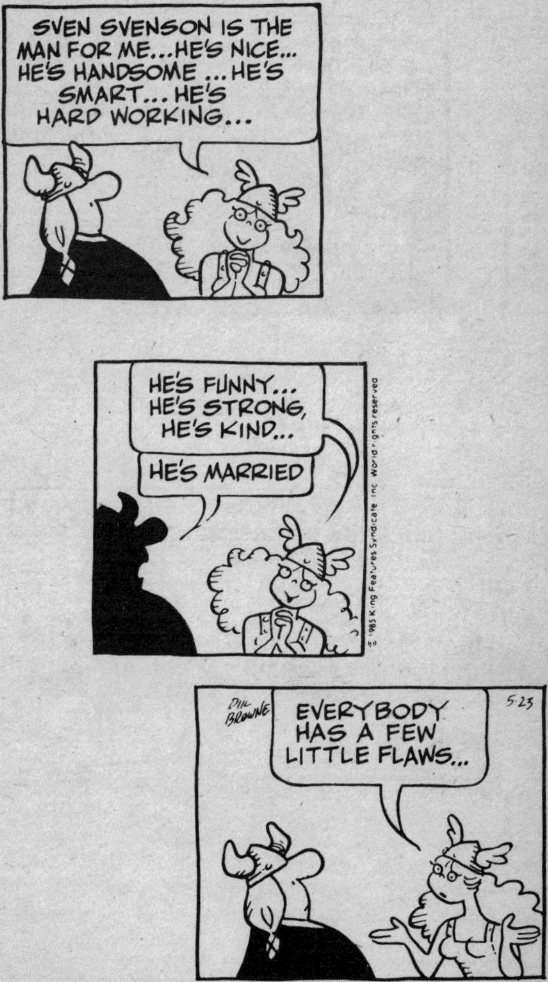
SVEN SVENSON IS THE MAN FOR ME...HE'S NICE... HE'S HANDSOME ...HE'S SMART... HE'S HARD WORKING...
HE'S FUNNY... HE'S STRONG, HE'S KIND...
HE'S MARRIED
DIK BROWNE
5-23
EVERYBODY HAS A FEW LITTLE FLAWS...

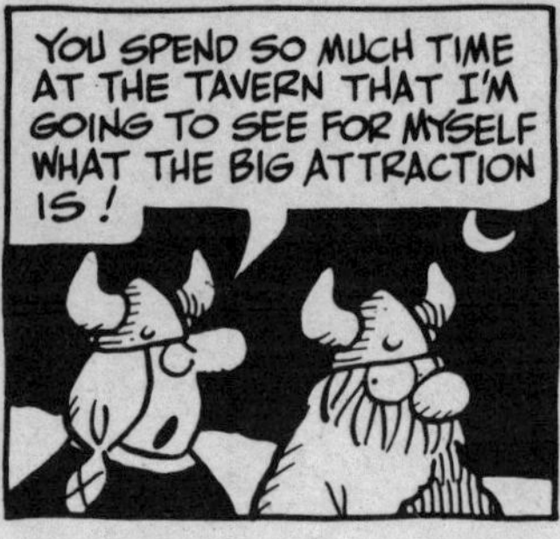
YOU SPEND SO MUCH TIME AT THE TAVERN THAT I'M GOING TO SEE FOR MYSELF WHAT THE BIG ATTRACTION IS!

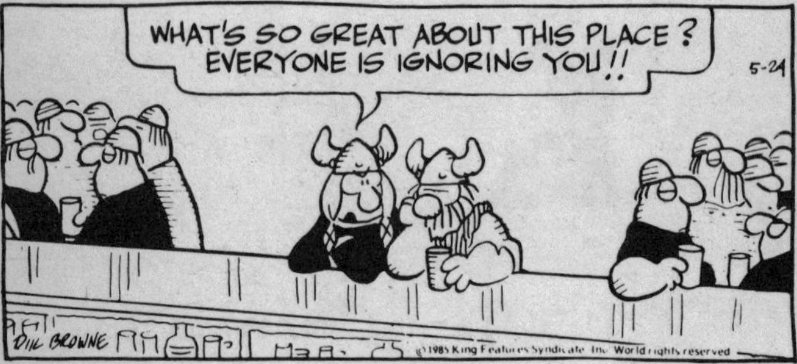
WHAT'S SO GREAT ABOUT THIS PLACE? EVERYONE IS IGNORING YOU!!
5-24
DIK BROWNE
© 1985 King Features Syndicate, Inc. World rights reserved

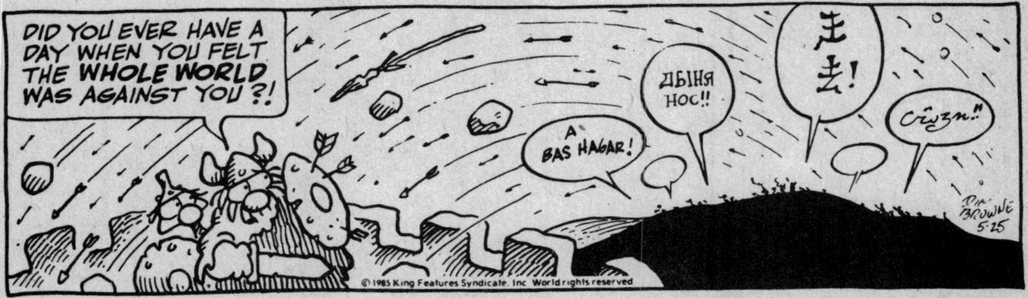
DID YOU EVER HAVE A DAY WHEN YOU FELT THE **WHOLE WORLD** WAS AGAINST YOU ?!
A BAS HAGAR!
ДЫНЯ НОС!!
DIK BROWNE 5·25
© 1985 King Features Syndicate, Inc. World rights reserved

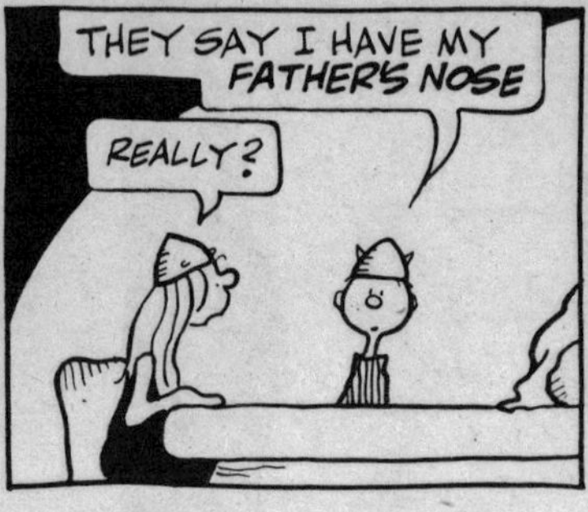
THEY SAY I HAVE MY FATHER'S NOSE
REALLY?

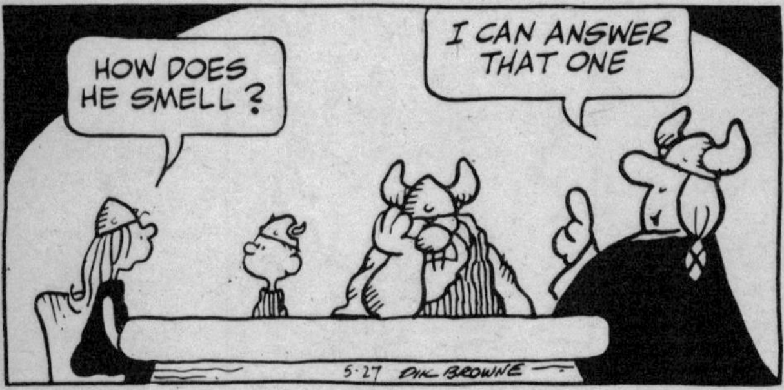
HOW DOES HE SMELL?
I CAN ANSWER THAT ONE
5-27 DIK BROWNE

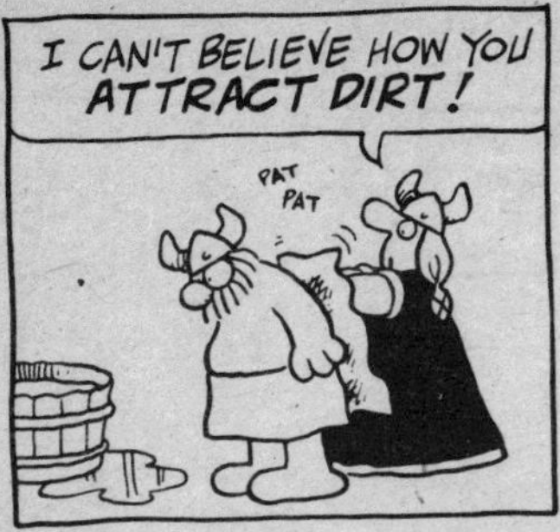
I CAN'T BELIEVE HOW YOU ATTRACT DIRT!
PAT PAT

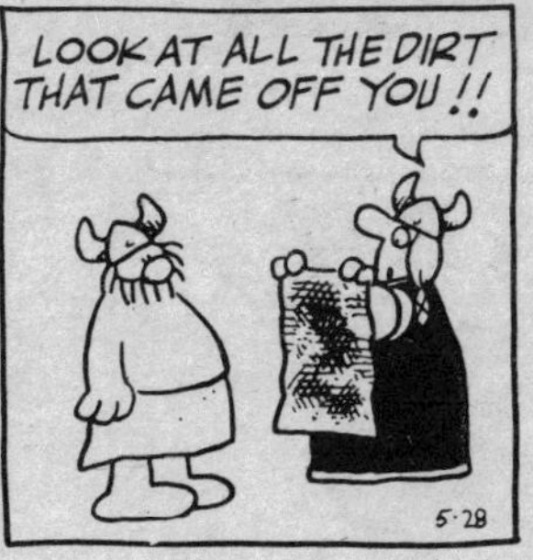
LOOK AT ALL THE DIRT THAT CAME OFF YOU!!
5-28

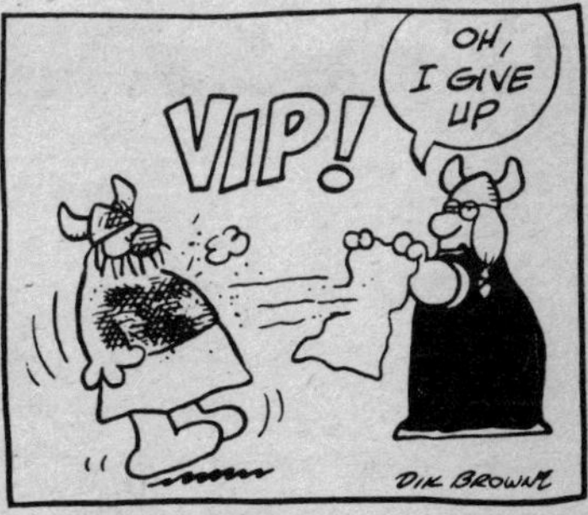
VIP!
OH, I GIVE UP
DIK BROWNE

FETCH MY SLIPPERS, SNERT!
KA-POP!
DIK BROWNE 5-29
AND THAT'S MY BEST FRIEND?

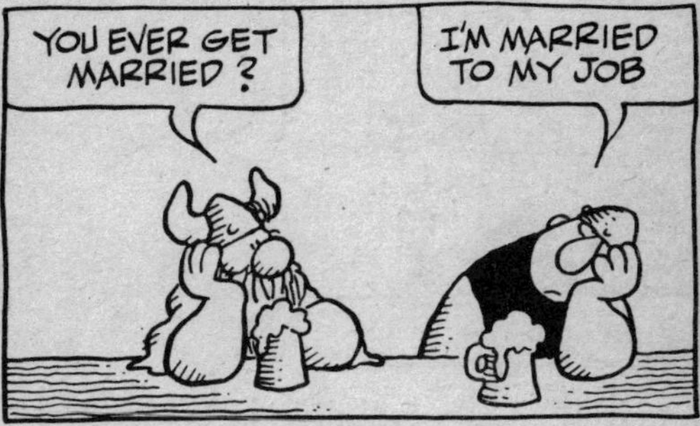
YOU EVER GET MARRIED ?
I'M MARRIED TO MY JOB

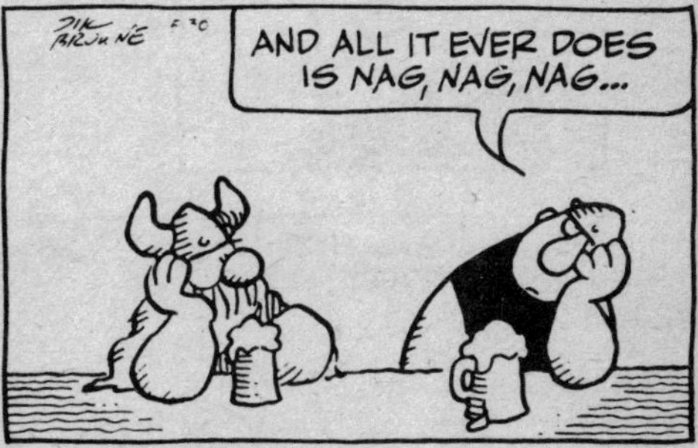
AND ALL IT EVER DOES IS NAG, NAG, NAG...

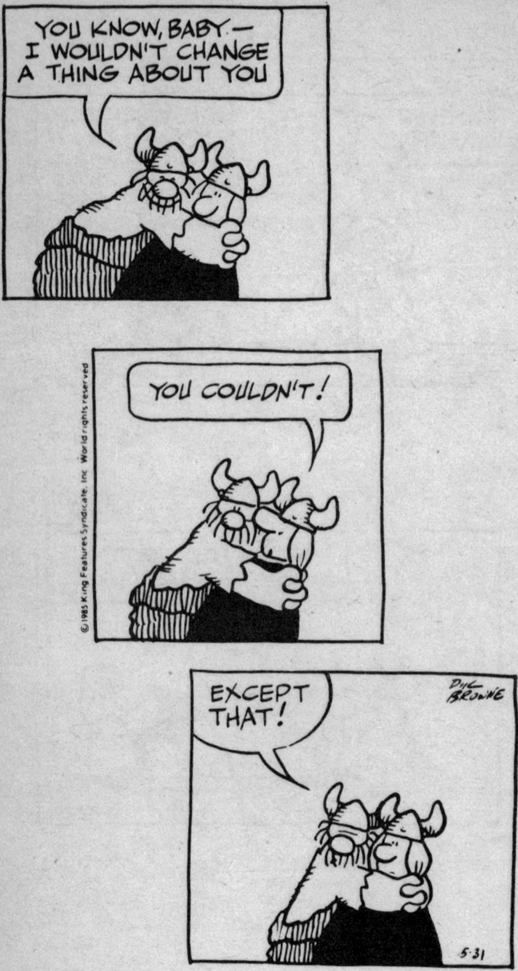
YOU KNOW, BABY —
I WOULDN'T CHANGE
A THING ABOUT YOU
YOU COULDN'T!
EXCEPT
THAT!
DIK BROWNE
5·31

HI, HAGAR. ARE YOU ALONE?
NOT ANYMORE..
6-1
DIK BROWNE

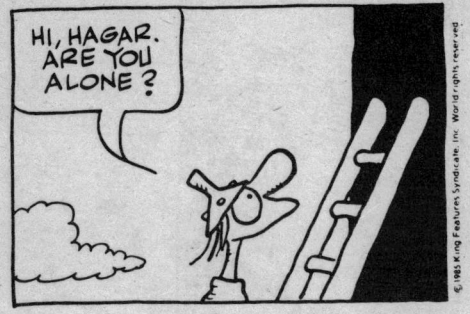

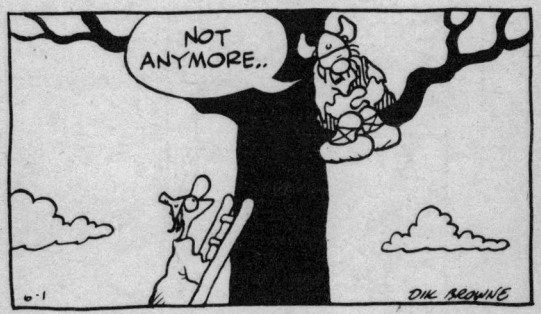

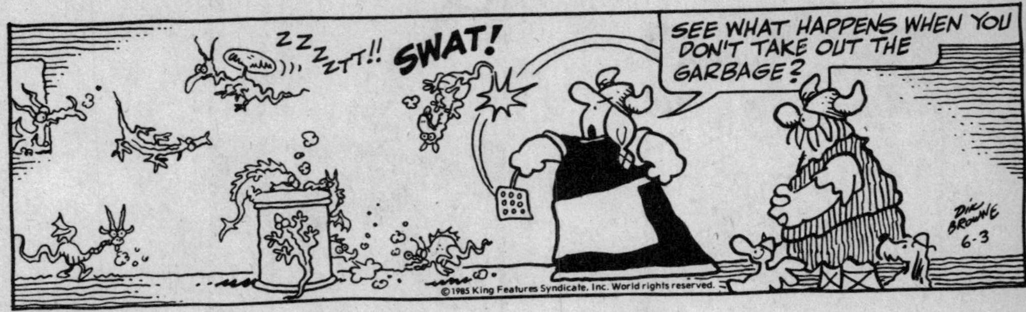
ZZZZTT!!
SWAT!
SEE WHAT HAPPENS WHEN YOU DON'T TAKE OUT THE GARBAGE?
DIK BROWNE 6-3
©1985 King Features Syndicate, Inc. World rights reserved.

HAMLET, WILL YOU FIX THE SUNDIAL ?
SURE, MOM
HE'S THE ONLY ONE WHO'S MECHANICALLY INCLINED IN OUR FAMILY
KICK!
6-4
DIK BROWNE

YOU HAVE TO GO ON A DIET
I WANT A SECOND OPINION
DIK BROWNE 6-5

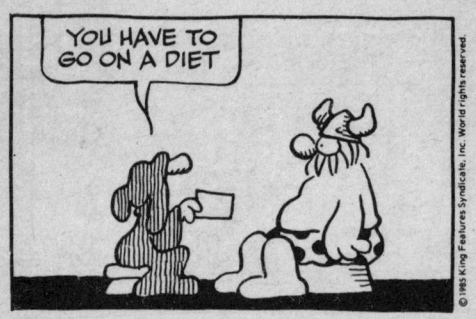

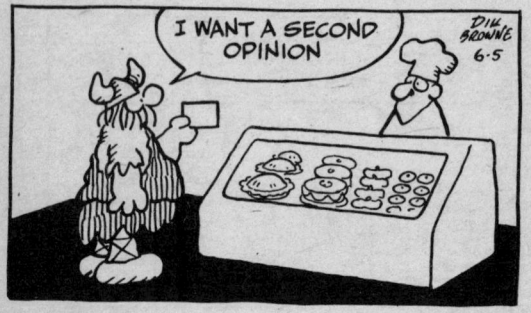

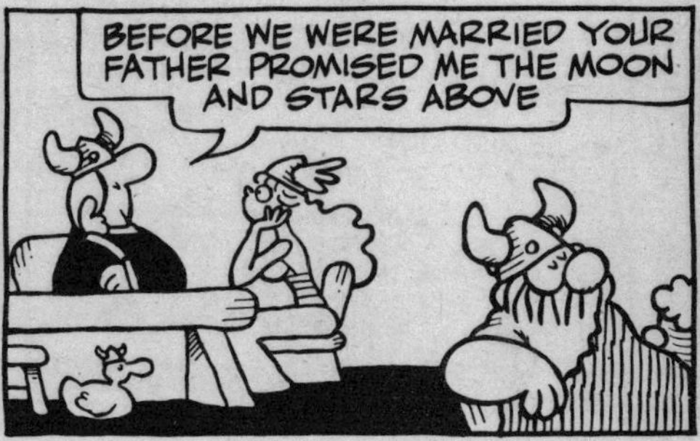
BEFORE WE WERE MARRIED YOUR FATHER PROMISED ME THE MOON AND STARS ABOVE

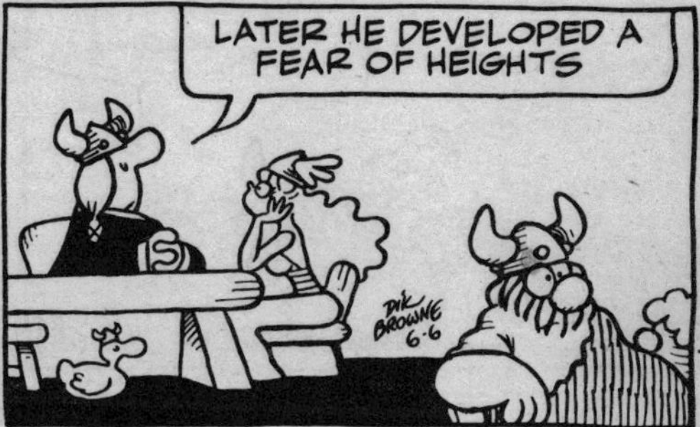
LATER HE DEVELOPED A FEAR OF HEIGHTS
DIK BROWNE 6-6

WHAT'LL YOU HAVE?
TWO BEERS.
AND I'LL HAVE THE SAME!
DIK BROWNE 6-7
DID I SAY SOMETHING WRONG?

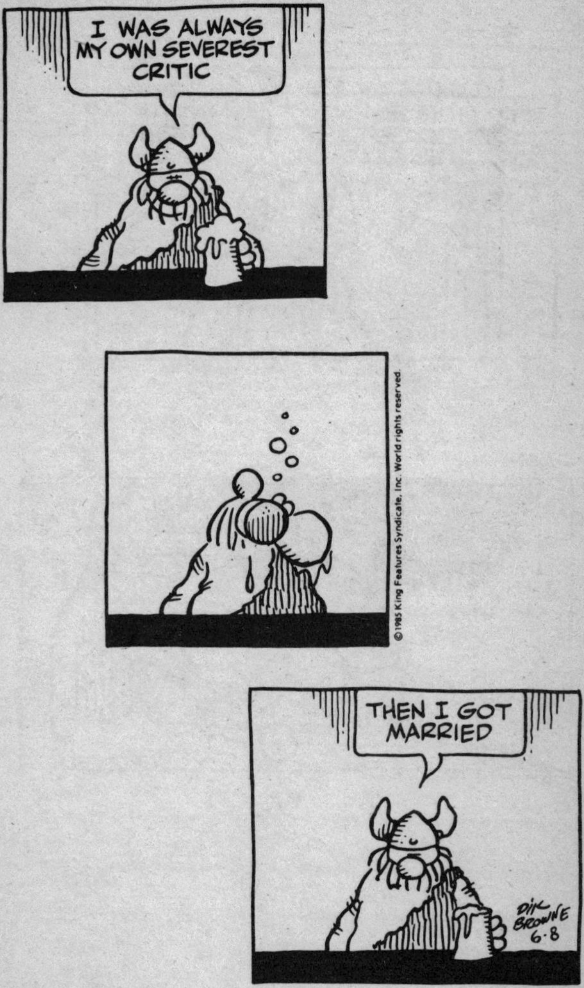
I WAS ALWAYS MY OWN SEVEREST CRITIC
THEN I GOT MARRIED
DIK BROWNE 6·8

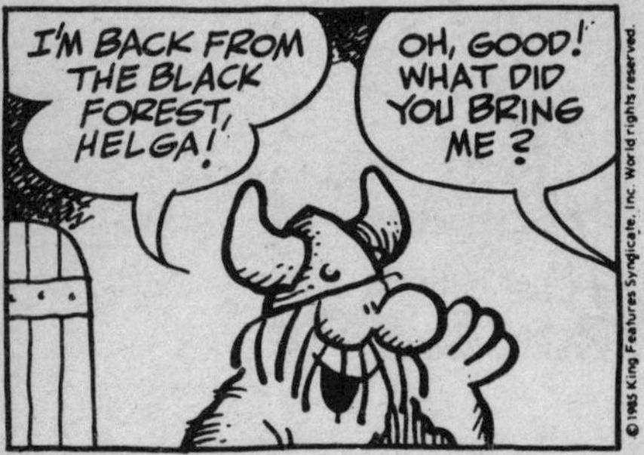
I'M BACK FROM THE BLACK FOREST, HELGA!
OH, GOOD! WHAT DID YOU BRING ME?
© 1985 King Features Syndicate, Inc. World rights reserved.

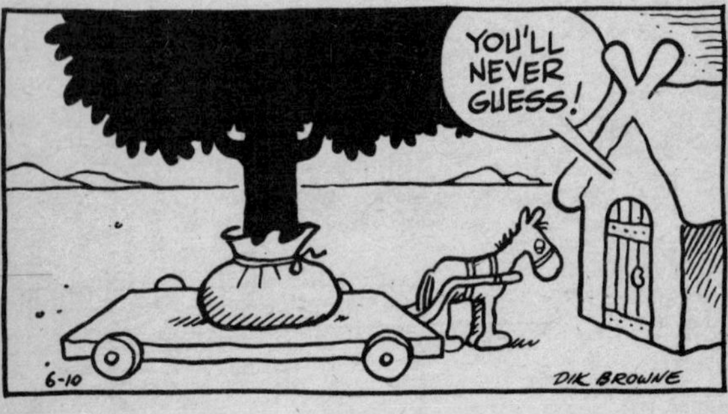
YOU'LL NEVER GUESS!
6-10
DIK BROWNE

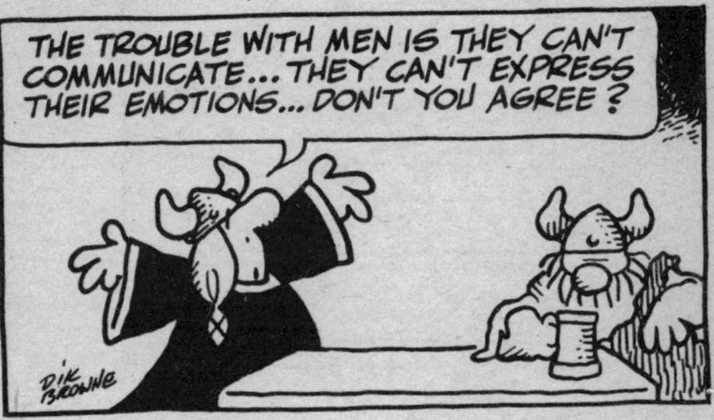
THE TROUBLE WITH MEN IS THEY CAN'T COMMUNICATE... THEY CAN'T EXPRESS THEIR EMOTIONS... DON'T YOU AGREE?
DIK BROWNE

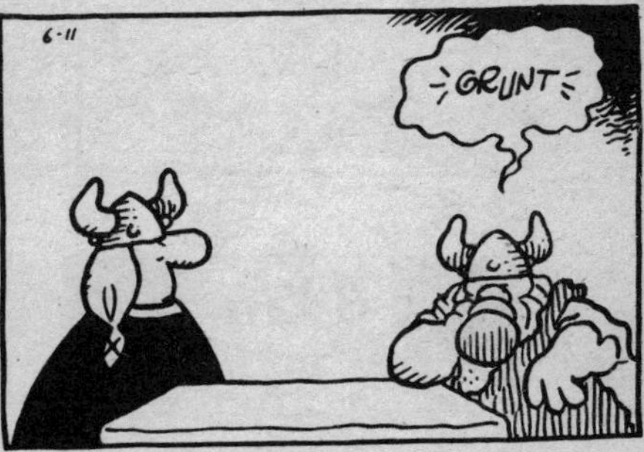
6-11
GRUNT

AH!
BAM!
© 1985 King Features Syndicate, Inc. World rights reserved
AW!...
DIK BROWNE
6-12

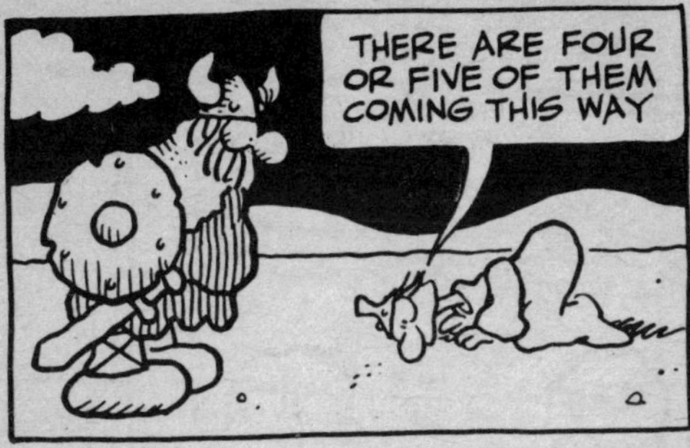
THERE ARE FOUR OR FIVE OF THEM COMING THIS WAY

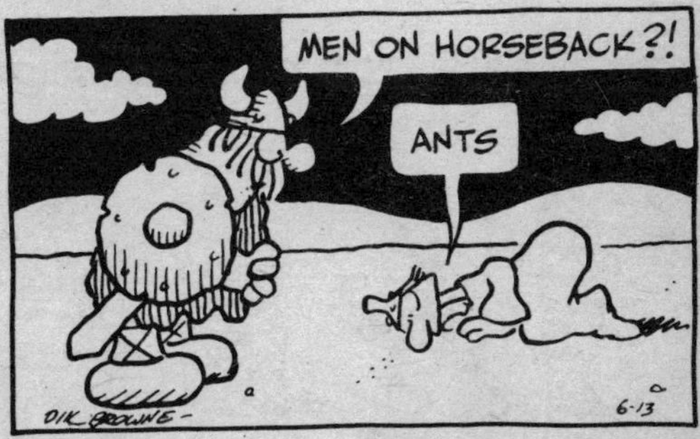
MEN ON HORSEBACK?!
ANTS
DIK BROWNE
6-13

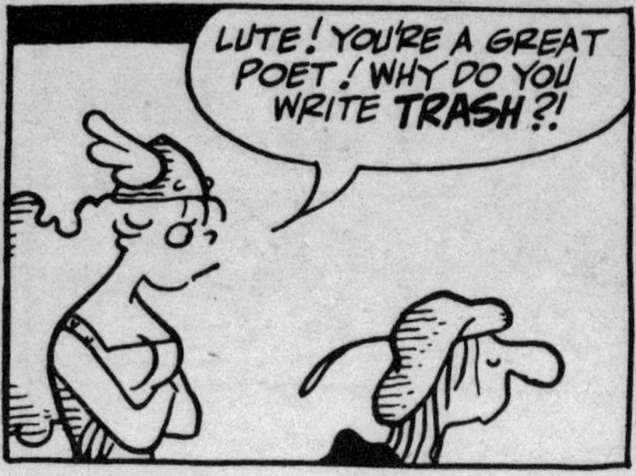

LUTE! YOU'RE A GREAT POET! WHY DO YOU WRITE TRASH?!

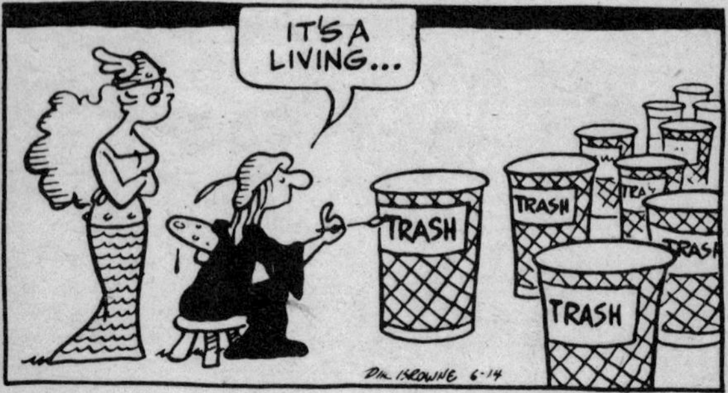

IT'S A LIVING...
TRASH
TRASH
TRASH
DIK BROWNE 6-14

I'M LEAVING TO SACK AND LOOT ENGLAND IN THE MORNING
DO YOU WANT ME TO PACK SOME EXTRA SHIRTS AND UNDERWEAR?
DIK BROWNE
6-15
NO, DON'T BOTHER
© 1985 King Features Syndicate, Inc. World rights reserved
I'LL ONLY BE GONE 3 MONTHS

THE QUESTION IS: DO YOU WANT POWER ...OR GOLD...OR TO BE TRULY CONTENTED?
POWER!
THEN I'D BE ABLE TO GET THE GOLD
DIK BROWNE 6-17
...THEN I'D BE CONTENTED

HAGAR, ARE YOU AWAKE?
Z Z Z Z Z
GOOD! NOW I CAN GO THROUGH HIS POCKETS
6-18
DIK BROWNE
YES, I'M AWAKE!

YOU WANT TO EAT YOUR CAKE AND HAVE IT, TOO!!!
© 1985 King Features Syndicate, Inc. World rights reserved.
IS THAT POSSIBLE?
DIK BROWNE
6-19

4000 SAXONS ARE 20 LEAGUES TO THE NORTH
ANYTHING ELSE ?
DIK BROWNE
THERE'S 20¢ DUE ON THIS MESSAGE
6·20

WELCOME TO MY HOME, HAGAR
THANKS, OOK
JUST PUT YOUR STUFF IN THE CORNER
6·21 DIK BROWNE

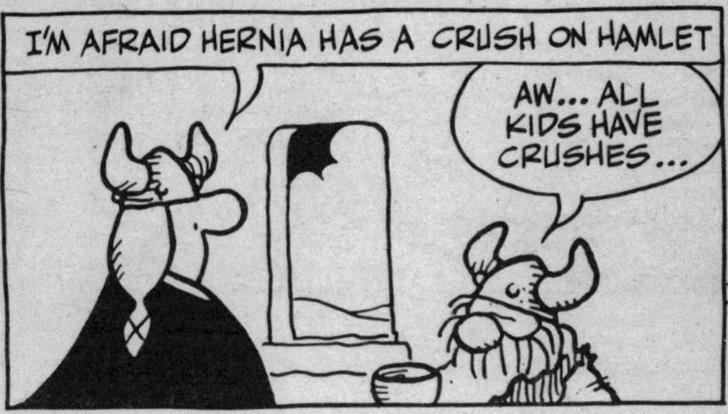
I'M AFRAID HERNIA HAS A CRUSH ON HAMLET
AW... ALL KIDS HAVE CRUSHES...

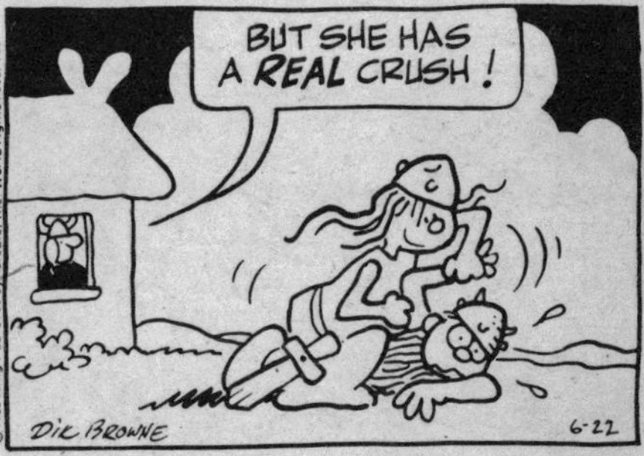
BUT SHE HAS A *REAL* CRUSH!
DIK BROWNE
6-22

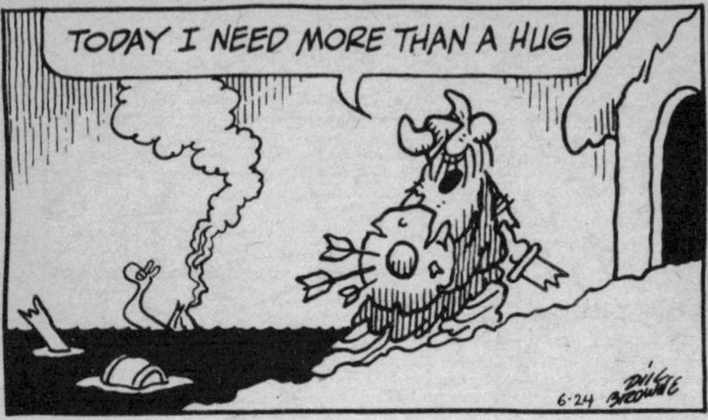
TODAY I NEED MORE THAN A HUG
6·24 DIK BROWNE

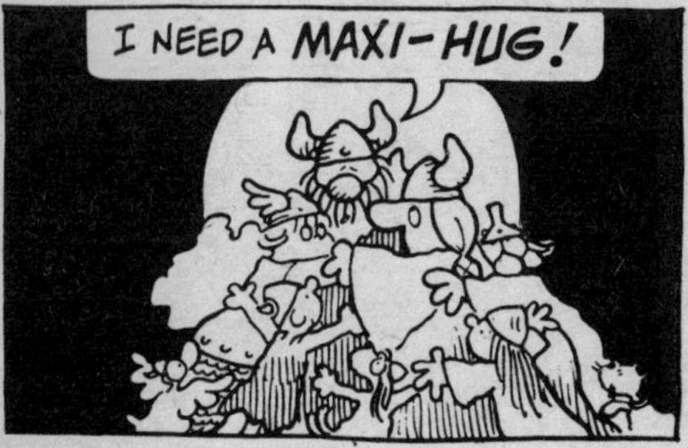
I NEED A MAXI-HUG!

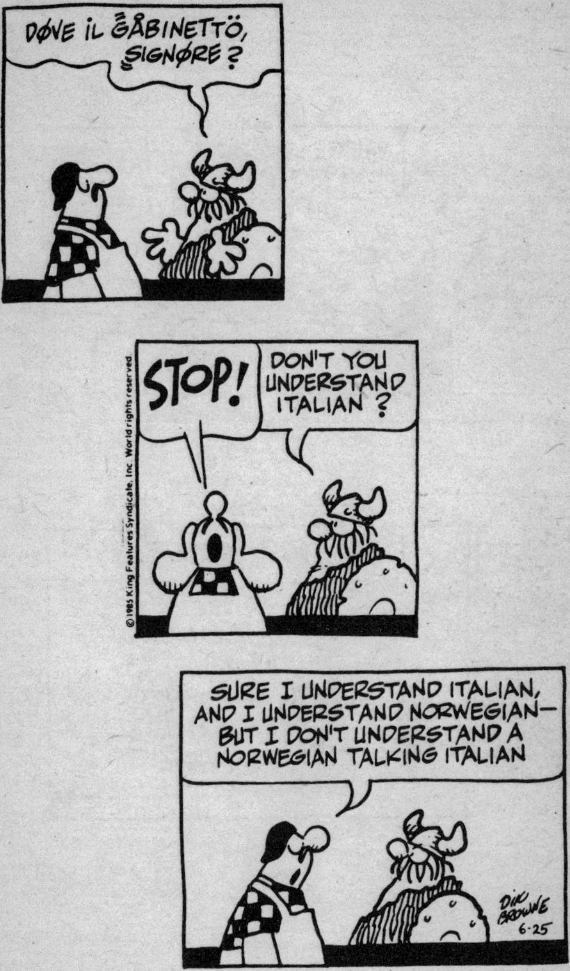
DØVE IL GÅBINETTÖ, SIGNØRE?
STOP!
DON'T YOU UNDERSTAND ITALIAN?
SURE I UNDERSTAND ITALIAN, AND I UNDERSTAND NORWEGIAN— BUT I DON'T UNDERSTAND A NORWEGIAN TALKING ITALIAN
DIK BROWNE 6-25

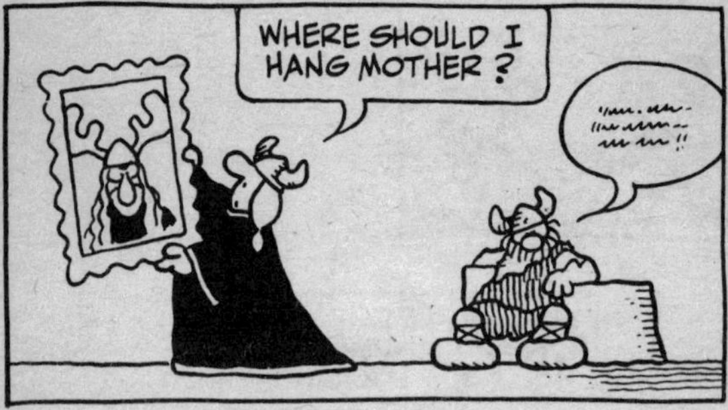
WHERE SHOULD I HANG MOTHER ?

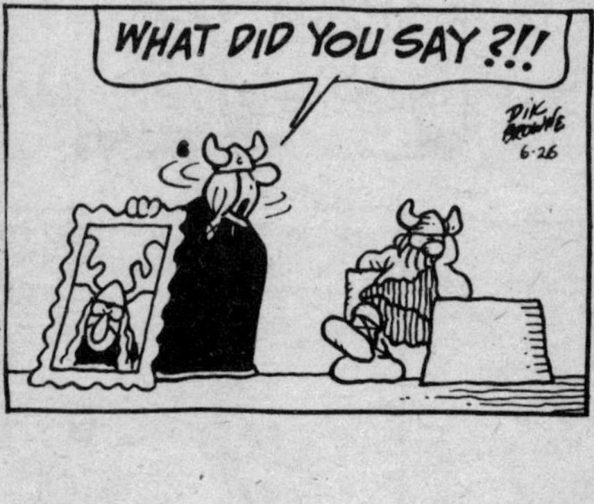
WHAT DID YOU SAY ?!!
DIK BROWNE
6-26

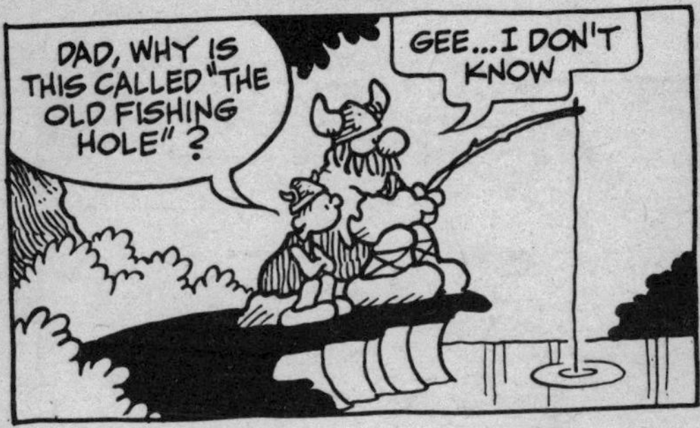
DAD, WHY IS THIS CALLED "THE OLD FISHING HOLE"?
GEE... I DON'T KNOW

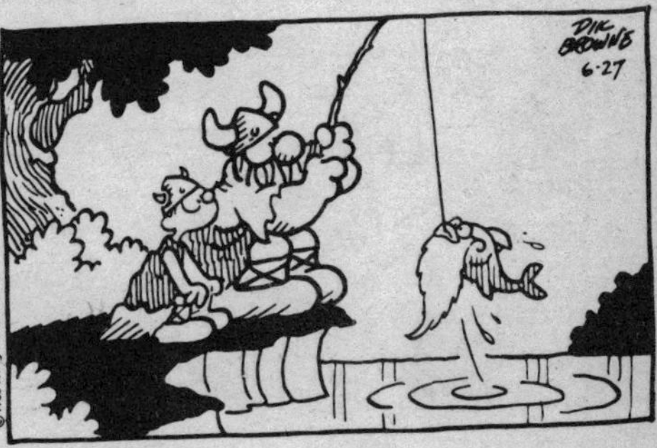
DIK BROWNE
6·27

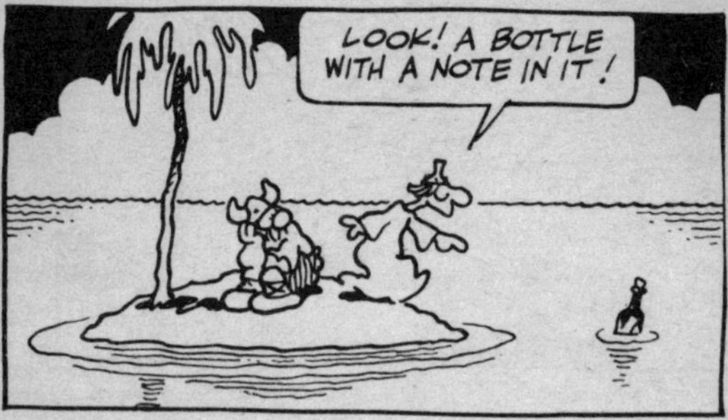
LOOK! A BOTTLE WITH A NOTE IN IT!

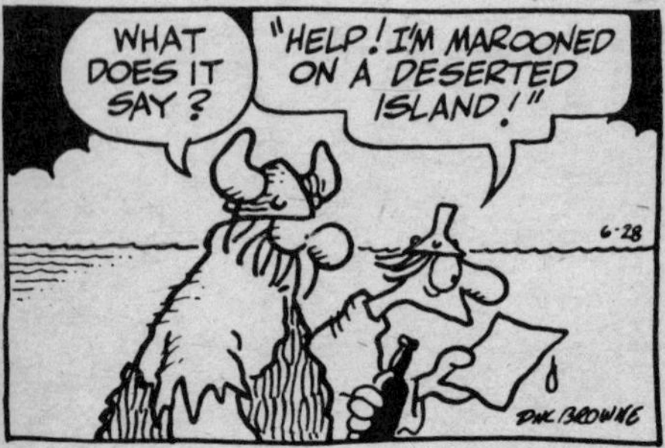
WHAT DOES IT SAY?
"HELP! I'M MAROONED ON A DESERTED ISLAND!"
6-28
DIK BROWNE

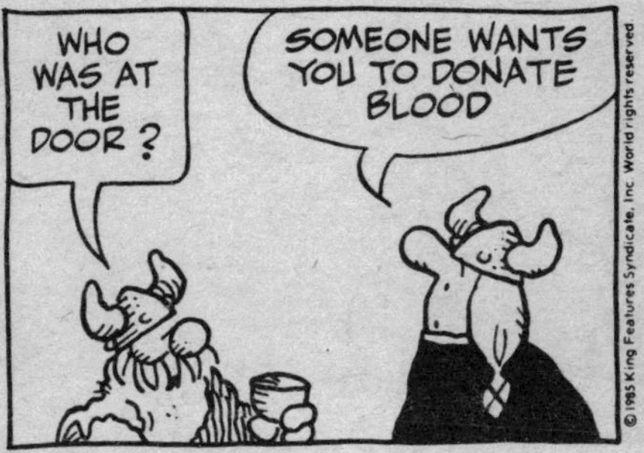
WHO WAS AT THE DOOR ?
SOMEONE WANTS YOU TO DONATE BLOOD
© 1985 King Features Syndicate, Inc. World rights reserved.

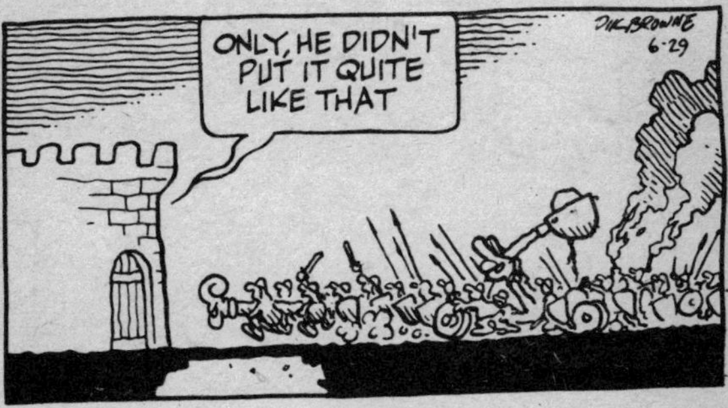
ONLY, HE DIDN'T PUT IT QUITE LIKE THAT
DIK BROWNE
6-29

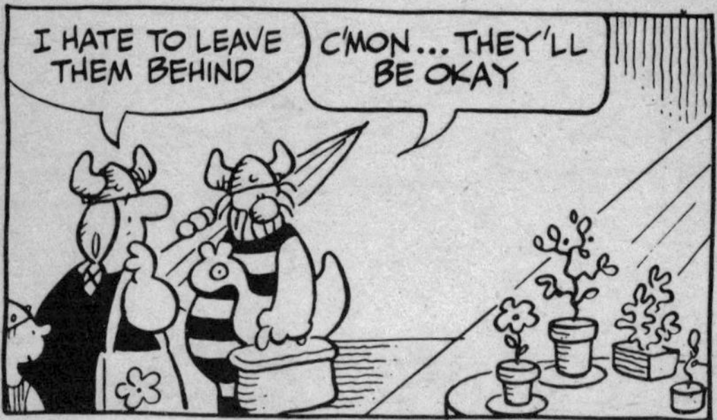
I HATE TO LEAVE THEM BEHIND
C'MON... THEY'LL BE OKAY

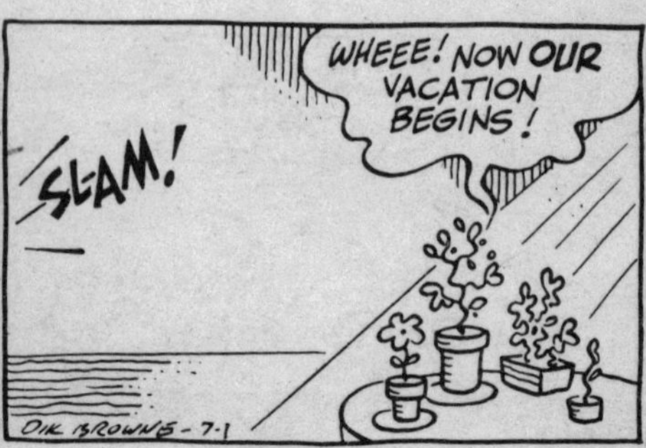
WHEEE! NOW OUR VACATION BEGINS!
SLAM!
DIK BROWNE - 7-1

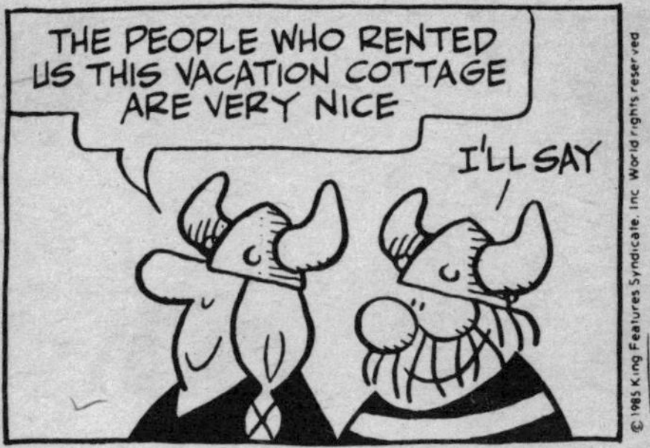
THE PEOPLE WHO RENTED US THIS VACATION COTTAGE ARE VERY NICE
I'LL SAY
© 1985 King Features Syndicate, Inc. World rights reserved

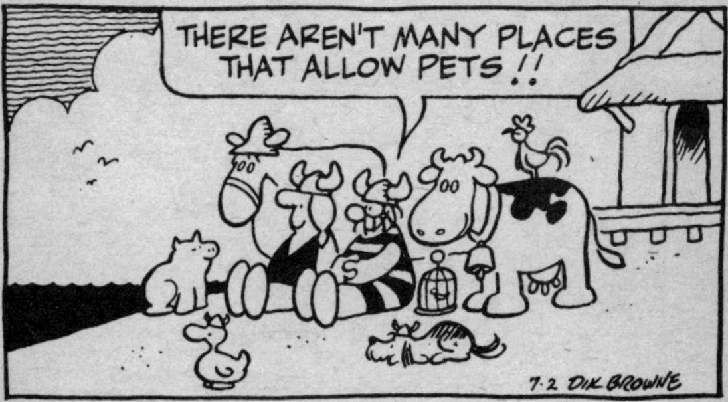
THERE AREN'T MANY PLACES THAT ALLOW PETS !!
7·2 DIK BROWNE

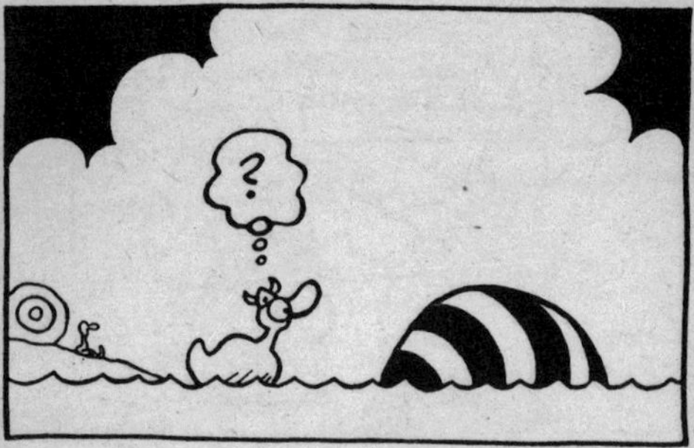
?

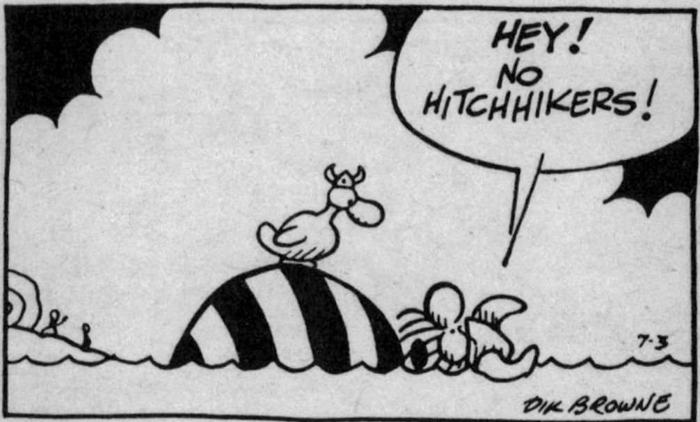
HEY! NO HITCHHIKERS!
7-3
DIK BROWNE

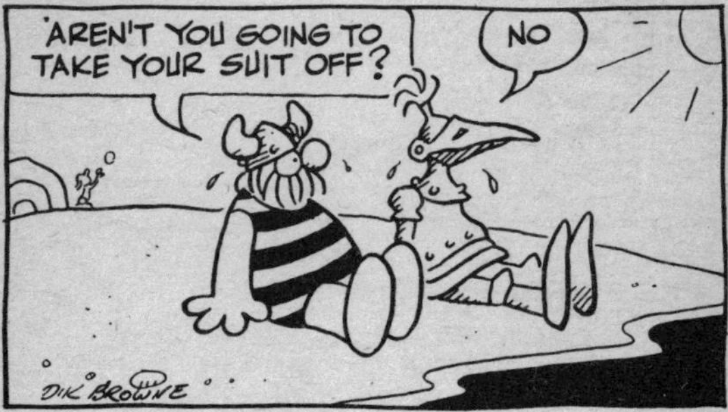
AREN'T YOU GOING TO TAKE YOUR SUIT OFF?
NO
DIK BROWNE

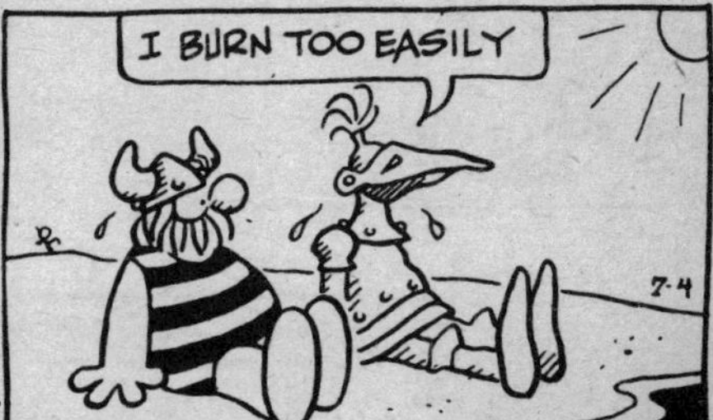
I BURN TOO EASILY
7-4

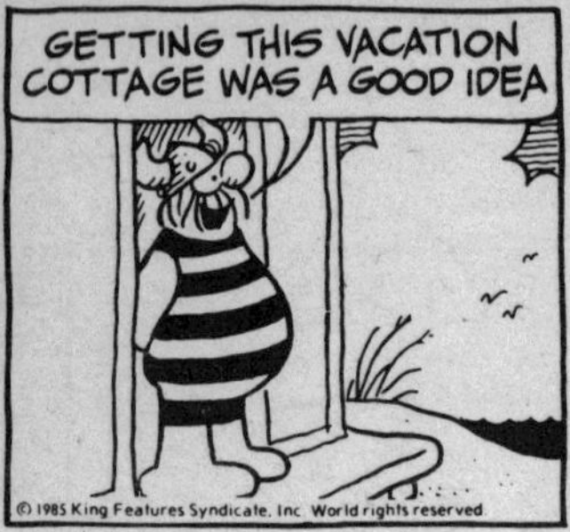
GETTING THIS VACATION COTTAGE WAS A GOOD IDEA
© 1985 King Features Syndicate, Inc. World rights reserved.

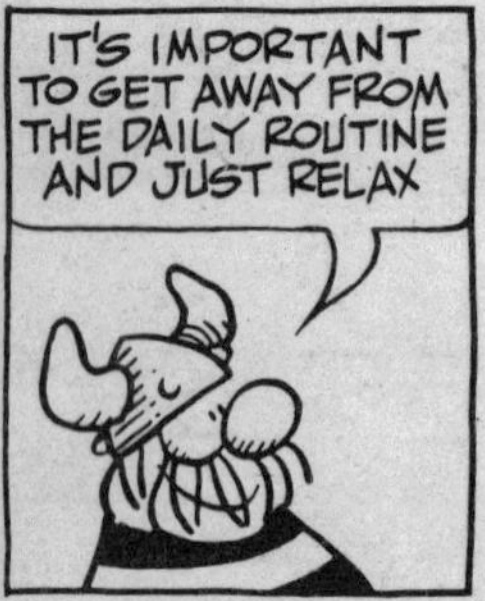
IT'S IMPORTANT TO GET AWAY FROM THE DAILY ROUTINE AND JUST RELAX

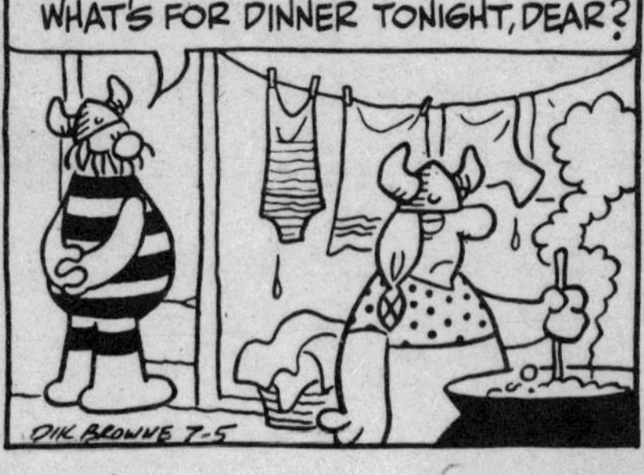
WHAT'S FOR DINNER TONIGHT, DEAR?
DIK BROWNE 7-5

YOU KNOW, THEY SAY MOST SHARK ATTACKS HAPPEN IN THREE FEET OF WATER
WHERE ARE YOU GOING?
TO GET A YARDSTICK
7-6
DIK BROWNE

PLINK!

THAT'S ONE WAY OF GETTING THEIR ATTENTION
©1985 King Features Syndicate, Inc. World rights reserved.
7·8
DIK BROWNE

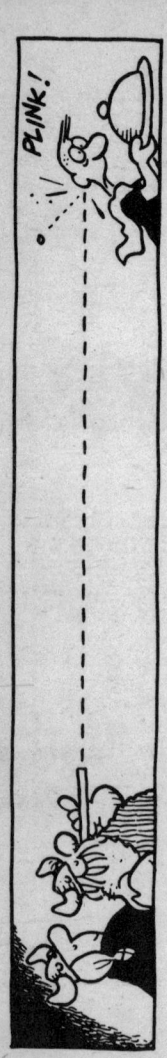

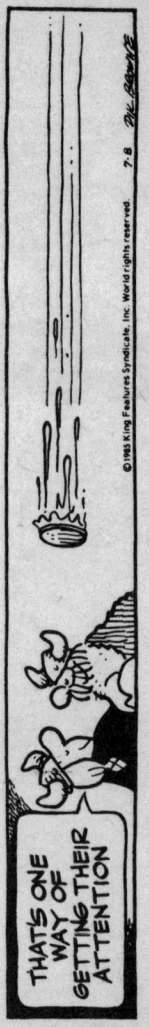

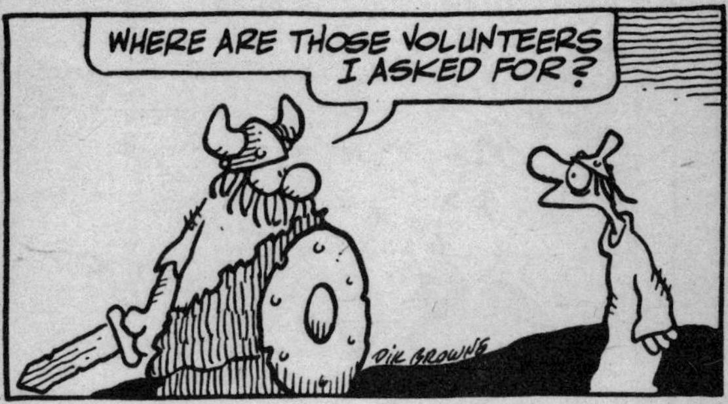
WHERE ARE THOSE VOLUNTEERS I ASKED FOR?
DIK BROWNE

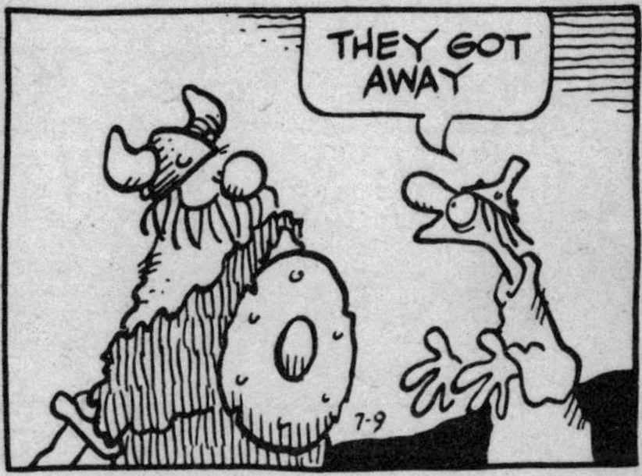
THEY GOT AWAY
7-9

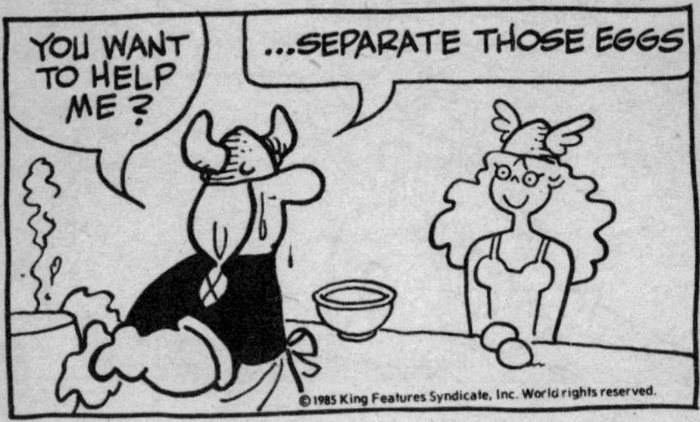
YOU WANT TO HELP ME?
...SEPARATE THOSE EGGS
© 1985 King Features Syndicate, Inc. World rights reserved.

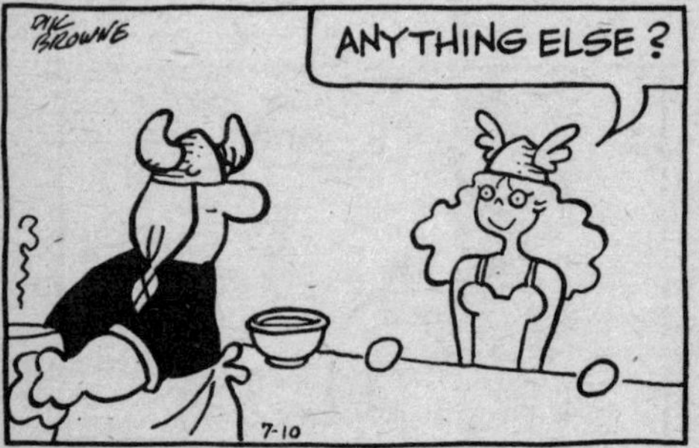
DIK BROWNE
ANYTHING ELSE?
7-10

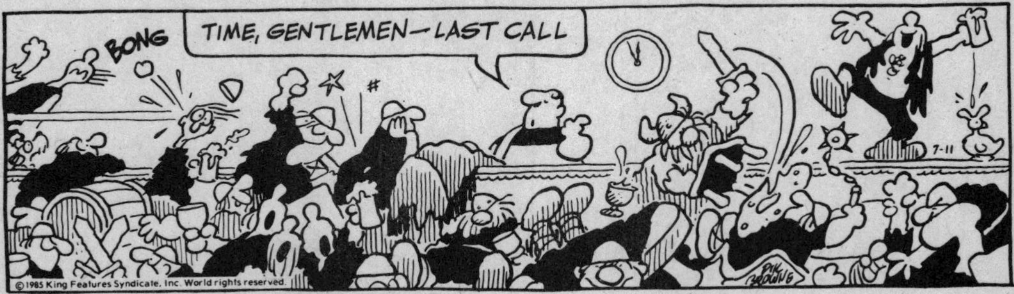
BONG
TIME, GENTLEMEN—LAST CALL
7-11
DIK BROWNE
© 1985 King Features Syndicate, Inc. World rights reserved.

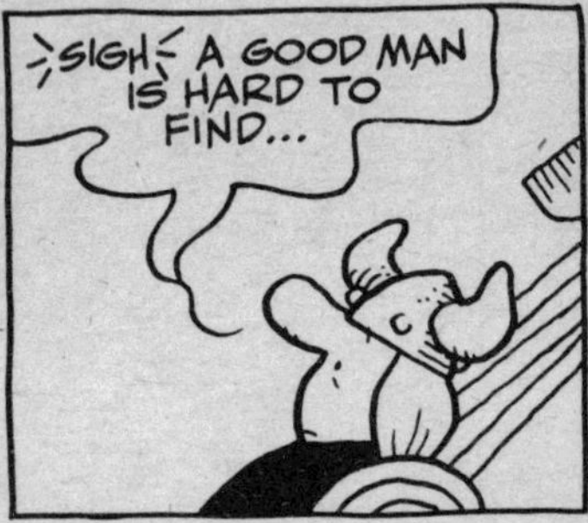
SIGH A GOOD MAN IS HARD TO FIND...

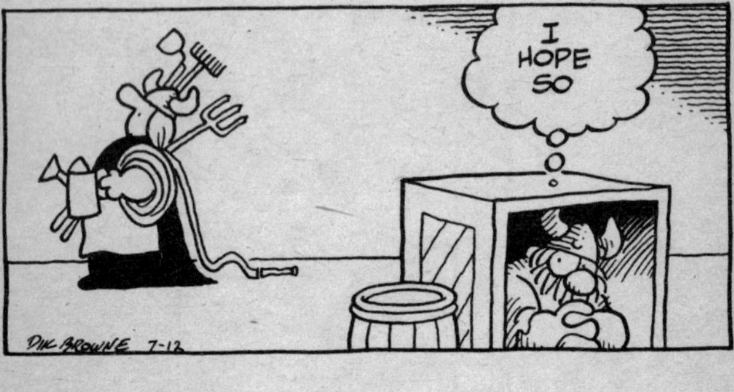
I HOPE SO
DIK BROWNE 7-12

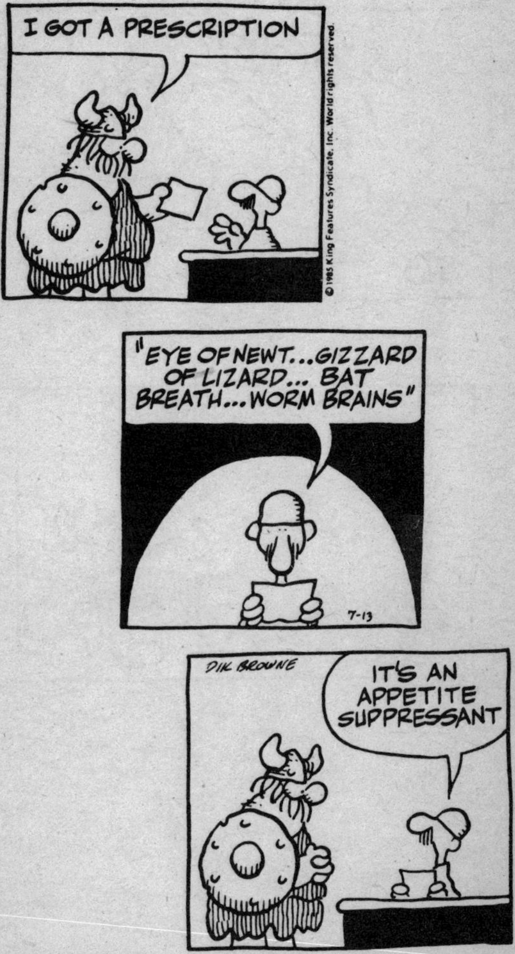
I GOT A PRESCRIPTION
"EYE OF NEWT...GIZZARD OF LIZARD... BAT BREATH...WORM BRAINS"
7-13
DIK BROWNE
IT'S AN APPETITE SUPPRESSANT

KVACK!
KVIET!
DIK BROWNE
7-15

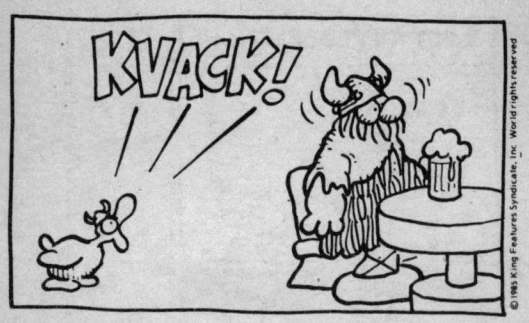

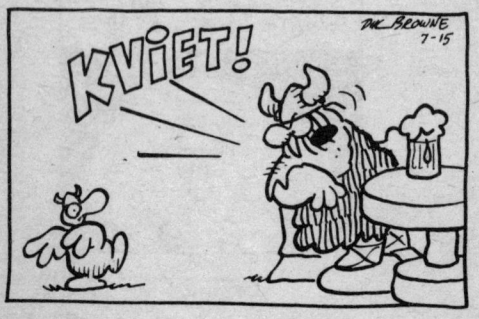